Fate's Palette

❧

Marcy Von Kohorn

Dedication

For Henry Von Kohorn
My Love Forever

Table of Contents

Forward

In the Beginning

In a way, I am a ghost writer. My grandfather, Morris, left a manuscript. It was handwritten on single sheets of white paper. My grandfather's handwriting was hard to read. His spelling was bad, and his grammar was worse. English was, of course, his second language, and he never went to school. The pages he left were not in any kind of order, and some pages were missing. I had to put his manuscript together like a jigsaw puzzle, which is why I procrastinated about writing his book. It had been passed down from family members, and what may have been his completed memoirs was now a challenge to reproduce.

But the one thing he had was his ability as a writer. I have tried to capture that in Part One, expressed in his own words. He was devoted to me, and I cherish his memory. For this reason and for his fascinating story, I am his ghost writer, and he is my beloved ghost who has been an important part of my life.

Marcy Von Kohorn

Part One

Morris

Journey of Hope
by Marcy Von Kohorn

Chapter One

The Entrepreneur

My family left our little village in Russia hiding in a hay wagon before the dawn of day. It was my mother and father, my little brother, Abe, my two sisters, Fanny and Rose, and my older cousin Martin, who was always in trouble with the law.

We drove for a very long time without stopping. We were buried under the bedding and bundles of our meager belongings. I was eight years old. By evening, we reached a railroad station and waited and waited. We waited so long that we fell asleep on the floor. The train finally pulled into the station, and I was lifted into an open car as we huddled together for warmth. The sound of the wheels echoed over and over again for what seemed like many days. Hungry, we were given dried fish, pumpernickel bread and water. We arrived at a large forest thick with trees. I think it was the border.

We walked and walked, in the darkness of night, crossing a stream of water. Martin carried my little brother Abe on his shoulders. We then reached a small wooden cabin, bare and cold, isolated with reminders of nameless fugitives. We rested till morning on fragments of bedding that smelled of mold and decay, then walked some more. Somehow, we arrived in Liverpool where we boarded a ship. There I first saw the "horse car."

We must have been in the lowest steerage with small round windows. The only time we could see anything was when the big ship rolled over on one side, then the other. Soon we were all seasick. Oh, how terrible it was. Everybody with yellow faces, lying on the floor, moaning. Days passed, and the ocean became calmer. I then began missing Martin. I found him in a compartment, a girl on his lap.

Finally, after many days, the ship stopped, and a small boat guided us to the dock. We were all on deck, but we could not get off until the next day as all the bundles had to be searched. I remember that Mother had some jewelry which she hid under the kerchief on her head.

The ship slipped into a dock at Christian street. It was July 3, 1888. We heard what sounded like guns shooting. It was a little scary. It was the sound of fireworks for the Fourth of July. There were colored people there to help. I had never seen a colored person before. They were kind to us and gave us bananas. I remember too that it was the first time I saw a car with no horse. It was being pulled by a cable in the ground and carried many people. It was like a miracle.

We had landed in Philadelphia. By that time, Father was already broke, but luck was with us as Mother had some rubles. We moved into a house in a dirty narrow alley. The house we left at home was like a palace compared to this. A few days later, we found a more suitable house that was still pretty primitive. It was on Seventh Street. We had 4 small rooms on the fourth floor. There was one rusty spigot with no hot water, a couple of broken-down mattresses with so many bed bugs they must have all been married with children.

The people downstairs were very fine. The husband of the family, Tom, was a policeman. They had four children who befriended us and taught us some American words. Tom suggested to my father that I could go out peddling, and, in a few days, I had a stock of merchandise and displays inside a flat basket, which was as long as I was tall. It was filled with matches, shoe strings for a penny and two suspenders for 10 cents. In those days, we had no belts. I stood on the Southwest corner where McClosky's saloon was. My first sale was to the owner of that saloon. He was good to me.

It was September, and hot, but there was a corrugated iron awning that protected me from the heat and the rain. I shouted loudly, so that people going into Shnellenburger's new store could hear me. Soon I was getting lots of business. It was a busy corner.

It was 8 o'clock and beginning to get dark when my sister Fanny came for me and I went home. It was the beginning of a salesman's career for me. My sister was worried that my mother was not well. Mother was frail and often had to rest.

I remember the cabbage soup we had for dinner. I was so hungry.

My father counted out the money. I was told I made $2.17. I was given 64 cents, which Father said was more than some men would make in a day. I was not allowed to eat before I said my prayers. I sure did not pray with my whole heart on an empty stomach. Frankly speaking, I did not like to pray because my father was so strict about praying

After dinner, I went outside to the fire escape and sat on the hot steps. My legs were a little tired from standing all day. I sat there with the other children looking for a cool breeze. They were teaching me to count and to say some words in the American speaking way. Soon I was called inside and told it was time to go to sleep.

The next morning, I was up at 6 and started the morning prayers that father insisted be said aloud, even though my stomach was empty. My father was very pious, almost fanatic. If I left out some words, he would beat me.

I put on the Tfilin, or straps, which were wrapped around my hand and my forehead and recited my prayers.

After breakfast, he took me to the peddlers supply store and selected more stock. I had about $3.00 worth of merchandise, or about double of yesterday. I started shouting again, "Look here. Cheap matches, 2 for 5 cents, shoe laces, suspenders." Sometimes I would go into the saloon to get a drink. My throat would be getting dry. I would go in and out and no one stopped me. I stood up on the long rail in front of the bar and snatched some food when I was hungry. At times, my sister and one of the girls that lived downstairs would come and bring me something to eat. They did not know that when I went into the saloon, I snatched food from the bar.

Once my mother went for a walk to buy a few groceries. She passed a store window with some small figurines that caught her eye. She turned around to go back home and could not find the figurines, as they were removed from the window, so she kept on walking. She sat down to rest on a step and fell asleep. She was lost and very tired. When she woke, her groceries were gone. A policeman found her and walked with her down South Street, until she found my department store corner. I walked her home. She was exhausted. I then went back to selling on my corner.

It was now the week before Easter, and I added some Easter eggs to my inventory.

After we had a little money, my father started a new venture, so we had to move again. It was manufacturing clothes. All the operators needed their own sewing machines that had to be carried through a narrow alley and up narrow stairs to the third floor. Those old Singer sewing machines were heavy. During that summer there were over 40 operators. It was a "#1 sweat shop." Some of the women had just landed off the boat and were learning to make pants. Some of the operators who worked there became very successful manufacturers, and one started a modern Russian bath house. One of the operators became a well-known Socialist.

Chapter Two

Peddling My Wares

Years passed, and I was still peddling my wares. I was getting the items cheaper and charging a little more. Every day I was on the corner at 8 a.m. and home at night when it got dark. I made a little stand to display all the items and was increasing my sales. I had added kerchiefs with red borders and women's stockings and cotton socks. I remember in the street car someone said, "I can't see the boy." The pack was so big.

That car was being pulled by two horses. At the top of the hill, the horses stopped, maybe to get a little rest as the car was loaded with people, some even standing on each side of the running boards. I got off there. I was polite and let the ladies go first. I remember a woman saying, "Thank you little boy." All the people were nice and kind then. I got off in front of a blacksmith's shop where horses were waiting on the pavement for their shoes. I thought I couldn't sell them anything, no matter how cheap, but the owner of the shop turned out to be my first customer of the day. He told me to go down the street to where he lived, and his wife bought a lot more. She called other women and, before I knew it, I was almost out of merchandise. When I came home, I had pockets full of money.

One day, I took the trolley car and stayed on a little longer. I got off a little past Columbia Ave. There were rows of houses and many women sitting on the steps talking. I started selling and within a few hours was all sold out again. I came home and dumped the money on the table. My sister Rose counted it, and my father came down and took it all.

I kept on going there every day and walking further and further until I found that I was in Chestnut Hill, which was a very upscale neighborhood. When winter came it got too cold to go so far, so I started to sell nearer to home. I would go as far as Allegheny Avenue and walk south, so that when the day was over, I could walk home and save the fare. I was now selecting my own merchandise. My pack was getting bigger and heavier every day. I added rattles for children, caps and even guns and sometimes firecrackers. I even went out on Sundays. The only days I did not go out were rainy and snowy days.

Many Saturdays and holidays, if we were not working, we children and some adults would walk to the Delaware River to watch some of the boats coming and going. There were often some big ships bringing more immigrants who would someday become famous citizens.

The ships looked beautiful to me, and I fantasized about being on one. There were two, called the Sylvan Del and the Sylvan Glen that would carry the people to the Thompson Race Track in Gloucester, New Jersey. As we walked further towards the South Pier, we saw long wagons loaded with fruit and loads of tomatoes. The farmers would bring them to the market place there to sell.

We then walked towards Walnut Street, where there was a big boat that went to a city called Baltimore. People could go on that boat for an excursion overnight and come back the next day. It only cost $1.00.

Father's business was doing well, and the pants the operators made were selling fast. I was learning to make them too, but no matter how much I tried and how I prayed, my father still beat me. I could not please him. If I skipped a line or did not pronounce a word as it should be, I would get a real good smack on my head, face or shoulder, wherever it happened to land.

It was now 1894, and I was 14 years old. It was the day after Easter. Father had to send out bundles of pants to a place on North Third Street, a large building opposite the old Manufacturers National Bank. I had to go along with the express man to help carry the bundles and to watch the wagon while he took in the pants.

How well I remember that day. Saying my prayers, I did not

comply so well. Father must have had some disappointment and was angry. When I tried to skip some words, I got a good beating, and it hurt to carry anything heavy. There was a man who worked at the pants factory who knew my father beat me and befriended me. He was a socialist and did not believe in religion anyhow. He grabbed the holy bag with the Tfilin out of my hands, walked over to the table where the pants were tied up and stuck that package of holy Tfilin into the bundle of pants.

Jim was a big scrapping man. He helped me to carry down the packages of pants to the express man. I was frightened at what my father would say if he knew what had happened and did not want any breakfast. My mother asked me what the matter was. I told her I was not hungry. When I came back, I could not find the receipt. My father was getting ready to give me another beating when my sister Fanny called my mother from her nap, for my mother was very fragile. She told my father to let me have breakfast first. I then found the receipt for the pants and went out to the alley to follow Father upstairs to the shop to give it to him. The only entrance to the factory was in the alley. In the front was the gents furnishing store of Millers & Sons.

Also in the alley was a large iron factory that made corrugated awnings. My youngest brother Abe was there watching the men forge together an awning when one of the sparks flew into his eye. I knew father would blame that on me and that I was in for it. Abe sure had a bad time of it. It still bothers him to this day. We took him to the Pennsylvania Hospital, and afterwards I walked to the Delaware River and saw that big boat going to the nice big city of Baltimore. I pictured myself on that boat. I had no money (maybe 50 cents) but remembered that my sister Fanny put some money under her pillow. Often, when I came home from work, I would slip into her room and hand her a little change before I gave it to Father. I started to count some money but heard someone coming up the stairs. I took $2.00, ran into my room and changed into my new pants, which I made to use on holidays.

I put on a clean shirt, grabbed my coat and left with $2.50 in my pocket. I left a hastily scribbled note and walked to the Delaware River with tears blinding my eyes. The big boat to Baltimore was waiting there. I boarded the boat, paid $1.00 and sat down on a comfortable chair. I cannot describe the thoughts that went in and out of my mind, but one picture that would always haunt me was Mother and how upset she would be. I knew how much she loved me.

Chapter Three

Baltimore

Now I was relaxing a bit and watching them put on the last minute freight, large and small boxes and even a horse and wagon. I heard a bell to let us know that it was time to leave the dock. Oh, how my heart began to ache as I saw that gang plank getting lifted onto the boat. I would have jumped off if I could swim. I then began to look around and became caught up in the excitement.

There were families scattered as we pulled away from the dock and looking for each other. There were some young boys and girls sitting around, cool and comfortable, listening to the band. I watched the beautiful scenery along the Delaware and wished that someone would ask me to dance. It was all so new and interesting that I forgot I was hungry. Near where I was sitting was a family with several children, moving to Baltimore. Seeing me sitting alone, the lady offered me a slice of bread and some homemade jam. My, was that good. She was so kind and offered me another slice. It was delicious, and I felt much better.

It was a beautiful night in May, the sky a velvet blue with a full moon reflected into the water. Everybody was dancing. Waiters were bringing drinks, and some sailors on leave were necking with their girlfriends on the deck chairs. Some folks standing along the rail were seasick. There were colored lanterns lighting the deck like fireflies.

At about 8:00 o'clock, we reached the wide Chesapeake Bay. It was new and exciting to me, but at the same time in my mind I wondered, "Where am I going and what was my family doing?" I had said in the short note I wrote that I was running away, but that I did not know where and that I would come back some day.

I heard people saying that we were coming to the locks, but I did not know what that meant. It sounded strange to me. Soon the ship slowed down, and passengers began to line up at the rail.

The sailors in charge were directing everyone to move to the other side, as the boat was listing too much on one side. All eyes were watching as the ship was sliding into the lock. The passage was so narrow, it did not seem possible that it could get through. At times it seemed that you could actually reach out and touch the wooden walls on either side. Ahead, I could see the gates open wide with water rushing through the sides. It was an amazing sight to me. Then, like magic, the boat was lifted and sailed smoothly through the waves, the big wheels splashing and spraying foam over the front of the boat. I was filled with wonder.

I fell into a sound sleep. It had been a long day and a troubled one. I was awakened by the ship's bell at five in the morning. Everything seemed like a hazy dream. Through the fog I could see the freight on deck. Men, women and children, just waking, were getting ready to disembark with their luggage. I was thinking how lucky I was, for I had nothing to carry. As the gang plank dropped down over the water, the fog lifted and I could see my future home, Baltimore. It was beginning to get light. The crew called out "all ashore."

I walked down the gang plank, following the crowd, feeling disheartened. There was a chill in the air, and I was shivering, pulling my light-weight summer jacket around me. I had $1.50 in my pocket. I was on Baltimore Avenue. I stopped off briefly at a small breakfast café for coffee and a doughnut, and then followed East Baltimore Street to Utah Street where it divides the city into East and West. I stopped at a window where there were dishes filled with sandwiches, fruit, orange juice and, on a high shelf, a huge urn pouring coffee into small cups as a moving shelf moved them forward. There was a large sign that said "Horn and Horn." Above the sign was a smaller sign that said "Help Wanted."

As I walked inside, looking around, a man approached me and said, "Can I help you with something?" "Yes," I replied. "I'm looking for a job." He said, "Wait here, I'll be right back." He returned and said, "Come back at 1:00 and bring an apron with you."

I walked down the block past a large factory called Strauss Clothing Manufacturing. On the corner was a saloon. I went through the swinging doors. It was lunch time and crowded with men. I saw a long table covered with a red striped oil cloth. The table was covered with all kinds of food. There was herring with onions, lunch meat and rye bread, pickled tomatoes and all sorts of delicious foods. I walked around the table, following the men and helping myself to the delicacies. I then went over to the bar, just able to see over it, looking for something to drink.

The bartender was busy serving the men. A tall man with a big stomach looked down at me. I was still clutching two slices of dark bread with some scrapple in my hands. The man asked me what I would like to drink. When I answered "beer," he gave me a sharp, stern look and said, "No beer for you, little boy," and handed me a glass of sarsaparilla, which looked like beer. There was a clock on the wall, and it was nearly one o'clock, so I hurried back to Horn & Horn.

I checked in with the same man who helped me before. "The manager has not returned yet. Leave your apron and come back tomorrow morning at eight," he said. Now I was discouraged. I did not know what to do. I walked slowly in the direction of the dock, thinking maybe I should go back home. I was despondent and ready to give up. I kept on walking east on Baltimore Street until I came to the river. There I saw a theater. There was a sign over the entrance that said "Continental" and another sign that announced vaudeville, singing, dancing and acrobatic acts.

I paid ten cents and went in. I would not spend three cents for a bag of peanuts, thinking I would need a whole dollar if I decided to go home. I could rest in the comfortable seat. I enjoyed watching the pretty girls singing and dancing and the tricks the acrobats performed.

It was almost 5:30 when the show was over. I started to walk to Pratt Street where the boat was docked. When I got there, the boat had just left.

Now my heart was heavy. I had tears in my eyes as I watched the boat disappear over the horizon and up the Chesapeake Bay. I walked up and down the street, thinking of mother and of my home. The bright sunshine began to fade, and it began to get dark as evening approached. I tried to think of a place to sleep. I was afraid to spend any more money, for I only had about $1.20 left.

Alongside the dock was a long shed with a big wide roof over it and canvas curtains hanging down around it. I was hungry, but never mind. The night had turned chilly, and I needed to find protection. There was no one inside. Slowly looking around, I saw some large packing cases empty except for some burlap bags. I lay down in one of them, pulled the bags around me for warmth, with some under my head for a pillow, and closed my eyes to sleep.

I slept soundly until the break of day. I know there must have been river rats scurrying around during the night, and once, when I lifted my head, I saw some of them running in all directions. They were as big as cats.

Through the morning mist, I could see the big ship approaching. The gang planks were soon put down and passengers and crew were walking on and off. I walked up the gang plank to find the men's lavatory. I found some mouthwash and soap on the counter and cleaned up the best I could. I straightened up my shirt collar and pants and felt much better when I walked down the plank. It was then after six.

I walked back to Horn and Horn. The manager was there and asked me if I had an apron. I told him no. He took me back to the kitchen, where he handed me an apron and gave me a few instructions as to how to take orders. I was not to write down the orders, but to just take a few at a time and remember them. He told me to always rush with the orders and to serve them as soon as possible, to never keep the customer waiting any longer than possible. He trained me well. From that morning on, I was never hungry again.

I was kept busy and the day went quickly. A big man, with a scar on the side of his face, came over and said, "You can go home now, Sonny. You did well. Come back tomorrow morning at seven."

When I looked at the clock, it was 10 pm. A strange feeling came over me as I wondered where I would go. I then noticed the other boy who also worked there getting ready to leave. I went to talk to him. "Which way do you go?" he asked. I answered, "I have no home and no place to go." I then told him all that had happened to me and how

I ended up in Baltimore. He was kind, and I felt that I had made a friend. He told me to come home with him and that he would talk to his mother.

We walked together east on Baltimore street. We passed the theater I had visited last night and turned left on High Street to his house. When he told his mother that I had left my home and family and had nowhere to go, I will never forget her answer. "I pity your poor mother," she said. At these words, I broke down in tears. She put her arms around me and tried to comfort me. "It's all right," she said. "You can stay here and sleep in Sammy's room. We are glad to have you."

My friend Sam and I went to his room. I did not even know his name until then. It was a small attic room on the 4th floor, but wonderfully clean, which was so important to me. We slept until 8 in the morning, as we did not need to report to work until 10. I went to a store nearby and bought a new shirt for twenty-five cents. I had received thirty-five cents in tips for my first day at work. Sam told me that we were working for Horn and Horn, which was the first quick lunch service in Baltimore. He said that Horn and Horn were partners. The partner who gave me the job later went to Philadelphia and started Horn and Hardarts. He was the one with the scar on his cheek, which I learned was from cancer. The other Horn branched out in Chicago, but the day I applied for a job was opening day at their first restaurant. I would be 15 this coming November.

I continued working at Horn and Horn for the entire summer. I earned $3.00 a week, in addition to tips and all I could eat. The only expenses I had were 50 cents a week for room rent and a small amount for clothing. I had no other friends, until I met some other boys who were of the dancing school crowd. They introduced me to the dancing academy near where I was living. I soon became an enthusiast and spent all my spare time in dancing school instead of a school of learning. I regretted all my life that I never had an education.

I soon became the best waltzer on the floor, and the girls were all eager to dance with me. I became friends with boys and girls of good families and was invited to their homes and to parties and evening gatherings, while other children of my age pursued an education.

After a while, I left Horn and Horn and took a job at a custom tailor making pants. The shop advertised "pants ordered today can be worn tomorrow."

One of my new friends was working at a shoe store on Saturday afternoon till 9, and he got me a job there selling shoes and rubbers. I made $2.00 a day there. I suggested to the boss that he should charge a little more and raise our salaries, so we then got $3.00 a day. It was easy work, and I was also making pants for the tailor shop.

Now I was able to save some money and still had time to go dancing.

Chapter Four

Atlantic City

Another winter and spring passed, and the summer excursions started. The tailor shop became very busy making white flannel pants, which were the fashion of the day. One day, one of our customers requested that I make a pair for him, with two hip pockets in back in addition to the usual ones on the side, and he wanted them on the same day. He was so pleased with his custom-made pants that he gave me a ticket on an excursion train to Atlantic City for Sunday. I boarded the train at 6 am. I wore my white flannel pants and a white silk shirt and looked pretty spiffy. I loved walking the boardwalk and watching the beautiful ocean and all the tourists on the beach.

I returned to Baltimore, quit my job, packed a suitcase and went back to Atlantic City, looking for adventure. It did not take long for me to discover what I was looking for. I found myself walking onto a huge dance floor on Mississippi Avenue, where the train had pulled in.

I introduced myself to the professor and told him about my experience at the dancing academy in Baltimore. I told him that I was planning to stay in Atlantic City and needed a room. He referred me to a boarding house across the street, where I rented a room. I unpacked, had a good breakfast and then walked the narrow, rugged boards almost to the end. I rented a bathing suit and went into the ocean, fighting the waves. I followed the ocean, still fighting the waves. I followed some of the crowd, took a tintype picture with a

17

group and treated myself to a hot dog and a cool soda.

When I went back to return the bathing suit, I was relieved to find that my money was still in my pants pocket. I did not know that I could have checked them. I had my fortune in that pocket. I had earned $708.

The wonderful day at the beach gave me a good appetite. After a hot dinner, I saw some musicians playing and a few couples dancing. The dancing professor from the academy was there, and we chatted. He told me that the academy was having a contest later that evening. He said that it had been well advertised, that they were expecting a large crowd and that it would be starting at 7:30. He invited me to attend. I asked him how I could find a partner who was good at waltzing. He told me that there would be many good dancers there without escorts.

I found a pretty young lady among the group. We danced the Shutters, which is something like the jitterbug, so popular then. She was a good dancer. We also danced to some waltz music until we were the last couple on the floor. At 9:30, a judges table was set up for the waltz contest. I went looking for my partner and found her at the bar with friends, drinking beer. I hoped, when we went out on the dance floor that she had not had too much to drink.

We were comfortable and in step with each other, spinning around the room and passing in front of the judge's table. The professor and his assistant kept walking around the floor, eliminating other couples until there were only three couples left. The music stopped. My partner and I were called to the platform and given first prize. The judge pinned a metal on my partner and handed me a five-dollar gold piece, while the audience erupted in a spontaneous applause. In the excitement of the moment, my partner disappeared with her friends, and, in bewilderment, I stood there holding the gold piece. Sadly, I never saw that lovely girl again. I cherished that award and later in my life gave it to the sunshine girl I married.

The next morning, I continued to explore my new home. Walking aimlessly, I came to Atlantic Avenue, where I saw the Pennsylvania Railroad Station, and, across the street, a long low building with a veranda in front, surrounded by flowers and trees and a large sign announcing "Schaeffer's Gardens." It was noon, so I went in for a beer (no questions asked) and helped myself to a buffet lunch.

As I was leaving, I saw a band of musicians. I stopped in front of the drummer and asked if they were having a parade. "No," he answered, "this is the Sousa Band." Soon after, a carriage pulled up in front of the open porch and a distinguished man got out. He had a little goatee and was very handsome. All the band members stood at attention as this famous band leader, Sousa, walked in, medals on his chest, standing straight and tall like a general. He walked into a large, beautiful garden with his men following onto a round, exquisitely decorated platform. There were hundreds of tables and chairs surrounded with banners and flowers. There were waiters with white coats and aprons and people flooding in to be seated as close to the bandstand as possible. A trumpet sounded, and everyone stood up as Sousa walked from a door in the rear, baton in hand. The band played our beloved anthem, "The Star-Spangled Banner."

The waiters were hurrying in and out of the bar, carrying large trays loaded with bottles of beer, wine and champagne. I stopped a waiter to ask who I could see for a job. He looked down at me and answered, "What, you a waiter?" I then saw another man who seemed more like a manager and asked him. He said, "What can you do?" I said, "I can do any job you give me." He asked me where I worked before, and when I answered Horn and Horn in Baltimore, he gave me one big smile.

"You from Baltimore? Why, I managed Horn and Horn for a while, but then found this building and opened a restaurant here. Now wait here till I get some seats for this crowd. I'll be right back."

When he returned, he pulled out his pocket watch and said, "It's now three o'clock. Go home and take a rest as you may be up late. Be back here at 5. Do you have a white coat and apron?" I answered, "No." He told me where to go and gave me a note to tell the owner to charge it to Schaeffer's.

"Do you have any money?" he asked. "Yes," I answered. "I have over seven hundred dollars in my pocket."

He took me upstairs to the office and told the clerk to put my money in the safe. I kept seven dollars and also my gold piece. I went to get my coat and apron and then back to my room for a badly needed nap. When I went back, right on time, Jim was looking for me, as he said there were so many people coming from the Gloucester races on the train that they were very busy.

"Now put on your coat and your apron, and I'll tell you how to take an order." "Never mind," I said. "I'll be fine."

I was assigned tables #10 to #15. They were the best in the garden. Pencil and book in my pocket, I took the first order from table 14 for 7 beers, a bottle of wine and a bottle of champagne. I kept on taking orders for all kinds of drinks, some of which I'd never heard of, like Mint Juleps, Martinis and Whiskey Sours. I marked them all down in my book the best I could, although I'm sure they were not spelled right.

All the waiters would give the bartenders their order slips, but they could not read mine, so I had to holler them out. They would shove the glasses and bottles to where I was. After an hour, I learned how to beat them on the amount I had to pay. There was a man sitting in the middle of the bar collecting all the money and pushing it into a sack. As different bartenders were filling my orders, I would remove a glass or two off the tray and pay less than I should pay. I kept on rushing the orders and running in and out of the bar.

All this time, Sousa and his band played on and on. At midnight, the band stopped playing and the customers left. Jim came over to tell me that if I liked, I could sleep with the men in the quarters which the house provided, at no cost. Since the next day was Sunday and I did not have to report until noon, I preferred to be in my rented room.

I worked there the rest of the summer and made a lot of money.

Chapter Five

Returning Home

It was now Labor Day weekend and a beautiful sparkling Sunday morning. I had fallen in love with Atlantic City. I had a suntan from the hours I spent walking the beach. I marveled at Steel Pier, which had just opened, and I saw the horse dive through the flaming hoop. I had tasted the famous salt water taffy and ridden in the roller chair. I knew when the summer ended all the tourist attractions would also end and probably my job too.

As I walked the boardwalk, deep in thought, like a vision from my memory, I saw my sister Fanny walking towards me. I could not believe we could be meeting this way. Tears came to my eyes as we embraced, and I realized how much I had missed my family. We sat on a bench and talked for a very long time. Fanny tried to persuade me to come home. I had liked my independent life, but when she told me about Mother and how she had missed me, I knew I had to go back. I was almost late for my job at the Garden, and that night I explained to Jim that it was time for me to go home.

The reunion with my family was very emotional. They were astounded at all I had accomplished and especially at the money I had earned. This time I did not hand it over to my father. Actually, he was doing well and did not need my help. He also treated me with more respect. Mother was even frailer, and I felt guilty for causing her such unhappiness.

I tried a few jobs, but nothing interesting or with any future. I worked for a store on South Street, called L Mark, as a barker. It was a clothing store and a tall, slim fellow named Mark owned it. I stood out front enticing people to go into the store. When it was fairly empty, he would come out and tell me, "You can start pulling them in again." That was fun, but there was no money in it.

My cousin Martin came to visit and invited me to join him in a new business. As photography was so new, we formed a company called the Empire Art Studio. We took portraits, enlarged them and used crayons to give them a subtle color. It was a promising business at that time, and we were doing well, but our partnership did not last long. I had wanted to keep reinvesting our profits and to hire salesmen to expand, and he said I was too young and did not understand business. Martin was then 26. He never was one of my favorites anyhow, and, since we could not agree, we parted and closed the company.

Our last order was for two pictures for Mr. Baker, President of one the oldest and most prestigious real estate companies in Philadelphia. He took a liking to me, and, when I delivered the two photographs to him, he asked me if I would like to work for him as an office boy. He offered me a very nice salary.

It was 1895, and I had already begun to sell automobiles for two brothers named Charles and William Gerson, who had an automobile company on North Broad Street. I was making good money, but I liked the idea of working in a real estate office.

Baker had two partners. The name of the firm was Baker, Ingham and Hewitt. I was hired to do odd jobs. I carried papers in and out of the office, picked up lunch for the brokers and their clients and had various errands. At the same time, I learned about real estate and found it interesting.

One day, while I was coming back to the office, a gentleman stopped me and said he would like to talk to me. He introduced himself as Bill Burns. He was a handsome man with sandy brown hair and a mustache. He asked me to have lunch with him during my noon break. It was a cold day, so we went to Kelly's Oyster Bar near the building. Mr. Burns arranged for a private room upstairs. I was puzzled, but I stayed calm. He asked me, "Do you know who I am?" I answered, "No."

Then he took out a shiny badge and said, "Read it." On it were the words "US Secret Service." Then I really was frightened and wondered what I had done, but he patted me on the back and said, "Don't be scared. I am a friend." He asked me where I came from, and many other personal questions.

Then he asked me, "Are you a citizen?" I answered, "No, but I hope to be when I turn 21 in November." After lunch he said, "Come with me." He took me to the third floor, to the US Court House. We went in by the side door. I waited there while he talked with the judge. He came back, smiling and asked me if there was someone who I knew a long time. I told him that I knew Mr. McKlosky since I sold matches and shoe laces on the corner of 5th and South Street, near his saloon.

He left me sitting in the court room. It was about 2 pm. He returned with Mr. McKlosky in about half an hour. Mr. McKlosky came over to say hello to me. I could not figure what this was all about. I waited while the two men talked to the judge. I was then asked to join them and was sworn in as an American citizen and then as a secret agent.

I stopped in at the real estate office, told them that I was not feeling well and was going home early. I then met Mr. Burns on the street. We were joined by another man named Mr. Manushe, and the three of us went to the 4th floor of the Post Office Building, to a door that said U S Secret Service.

I was then interrogated for some time and sworn to secrecy. It was now almost 5 o'clock. Mr. Burns handed me a check made out to me for $5.00 and asked me to sign it. He then handed me a five-dollar bill and took the check back. "Now," he said, "Go home and go to a dance tonight, and mum is the word." I assured him that I could be trusted. He told me to come back the next day for instructions.

Grandfather Morris

Chapter Six

The FBI

I was told to go to the real estate office as usual, but when it was time to leave the office at the end of the day, I was to hide somewhere in the office until everyone had left and the office was locked for the night. When I heard a knock on the door, I was to let Mr. Burns in the office. He was accompanied by Mr. McManus and two other men. I still did not know what it was all about and felt that maybe I was betraying my employer.

At once, they started searching the rooms. They were checking every drawer and looking in closets and opening every book. Then Mr. Burns took out a large magnifying glass and began to examine the carpet under one of the desks. I heard him say to Mr. McManus, "Look. This desk has been moved."

They lifted the desk that stood on a decorative carpet a little larger than the legs of the desk. Under that carpet, they found a bag filled with paper money in large denominations. Then I learned what it was all about. Ingham and Hewitt were convicted of counterfeiting and sent to jail, although there was a lot more work done by the district attorney before the trial. I was paid $8.00 a day by check from the US Treasury, plus expenses.

I was then put on another case and told to be a peddler, like I used to be, selling shoe laces and matches and anything available in the market. This time I was told to go door to door, although the area was sparsely populated. It was about 10 miles from Dover. The people on the farm were known to be with the Italian mafia and known to be killers.

It was an old dilapidated farm house, down a long lane stretching nearly a quarter of a mile. The understanding was that if I did not come out right away, everything was okay.

It was about 11 in the morning when I knocked on the door. A woman answered and was interested in seeing my wares. It was easy, like selling on the street corner. I heard men's voices. They were coming from the kitchen or some other part of the house. I stood near a closet which had a curtain over it. That is where the guns were hidden, and also the cash.

About a half an hour later, five men rushed in the open door, guns in hand: Burns, McManus and three constables from town. They searched the house and found the men, who were caught by surprise and taken to the county jail. There were seven of them. I showed Burns and McManus where I thought the guns were hidden. Being an amateur with little training, I received many compliments from the home office.

I was then put on another case. There was a man they suspected of counterfeiting. He lived with his family at 510 Vine Street in Philadelphia. I discovered that they had a son about my age. I joined a dancing academy, and, through the friends I made there, I got to know him. As I was still young and enjoyed meeting new people, we became a little group. We crashed weddings and went to parties just to dance and have fun. I still remember that his name was Nate Spietzer and we soon got to know each other well.

I confided in him that I was thrown out of the house because I came home too late, and my father was angry at me. I asked if I could rent a room at his house, for $5.00 a week. It was a good deal for him, as money was tight in those days. He said there was no extra room, but that I could sleep in his room. I had his confidence. He was a nice chap. He did not know anything much about his father's business, but he did give me a clue.

He mentioned that late at night two men would come to his house to see his father. His father told him not to ask questions, but he was curious. One Friday night when I was supposed to be asleep, I went downstairs and saw a slight light creeping under the bottom of the parlor door. I peeped through the keyhole and saw Mr. Spietzer and his wife wrapping pennies in strips of newspaper. I never saw so many pennies in my life.

The next day, when I reported to the office, Mr. Burns had gone to Washington, so I told Mr. McManus about it. We could not find out where the pennies were being made.

I heard the men arrive the following Friday night, and a week later, again on Friday night, I saw Mr. Barker watching the house. It was 3 a.m. when two men came to the door carrying heavy satchels. The two men were followed, and they found that the pennies were being made at Christian and Water Streets by the Delaware.

Just about at that time, the Cuban revolution started, and I was put on the trail of some Cuban gun smugglers. There was a boat in the harbor called the Bermuda, loaded with guns to go to Cuba. My job was to find out where the guns were being stored. I traced them to a large cigar factory on 2nd and Walnut Street.

It took me over a month till I finally found the connection. Since we needed to know who was behind this operation, I was told to get a job on the ship as a cabin boy. I was on the ship for two months. It was during the summer and very hot. I gathered a great deal of information and slipped a note to an agent dressed as a sailor and standing on the dock where we came ashore.

The next week it looked as though the ship was leaving again and I was to be on it. A message was sent to me at the house, but somehow, I never received the message. When I went to the office the next day, I was reprimanded. I then received a letter with a check, advising me that my services were no longer required. It was the most interesting job I have ever had, and I was sorry. I also felt that I was not treated fairly. On the other hand, I understand that in that kind of work there is no allowance for error.

Chapter Seven

Meeting Mollie

It was the winter of 1898. I had wanted to venture into an area that was more developed. I did not know what I was looking for.

I went to New York City and then to upstate New York. Winter was brutal in that part of the country, and the snowstorms made travel very difficult, so I returned home. My parents were still living in the same house and were happy to have me home again. I connected with a dancing academy and quickly found a group of friends. I was very popular because I was a good dancer and always wore tailor-made clothes. I had over $6,000 in the old Union Bank and felt like I was a king. Little did I realize how poor I was without an education.

It was that winter, when I was "foot loose and fancy free" and my sister asked me to go to a party. I did not want to go, as I did not know any of her friends and thought it would be boring. I only went to please her. I went to the party alone, as my sister Rose had a gentleman friend who took her.

As soon as I arrived, I was ready to leave. The boys were dressed in stiff Piccadilly collars and the girls, though pretty, wore stiff, starched skirts and tight ribbons around their necks. I wondered how they were able to move and, of course, there was no dancing.

My sister came over to me and said, "Morris, come with me. I'd like you to meet someone." I was not very enthusiastic, but I followed her. "I want you to meet my friend William Diamond and his sister Mollie," she said. "May I introduce my brother, Morris Silver."

I shook hands with William and held my breath, as there in front of my eyes was a beautiful angel. Her skin gleamed with purity, and her dark brown eyes captured the depth of her soul. I knew at once that I had found my love. My life changed. I no longer had a wanderlust. Now wherever I traveled, I came home to my Mollie. I knew that I had to make my fortune to give her the stars and the moon.

Mollie was only 16 when we met. I was in my twenties, a man of the world. She had an innocence, a gentleness and an innate gentility. She was as sweet as a day in May.

We were soon engaged, but her parents would not permit her to be married until she was 18.

I bought a horse and buggy for $550. My horse was a little Mustang breed, and I paid $20 a month to keep her in Kimberley's Stable on Broad Street. I loved to drive my girl through Fairmont Park. Was Mollie scared when I drove fast! We went to Willow Grove when it first opened. We had dinner on Sundays in the elegant dining room, where Sousa and his band played. You had to be dressed in evening clothes. It cost $2.50 a plate.

When Mollie turned 18, we had a beautiful wedding on February 20, 1900. Our first little home was at 6460 Mountain Street. It had a modern bathroom with marble counter tops. We had gaslight and a lovely garden.

I did make my fortune in real estate. I had learned a lot when I worked for Baker Ingham & Hewitt Real Estate. It was too bad that they became dishonest.

There were very few real estate companies in existence. It was a new and developing business. Land was cheap, and there were large parcels available that developers could build on or sometimes sell off part of the land.

Steel had recently been invented, and elevators were being built, which allowed for office buildings and apartment houses. The city undertook the construction of City Hall, but because of graft and corruption, it took 23 years to build. In 1886, it was the tallest building in Philadelphia. Elegant department stores like Wanamaker's, Gimbels and Strawbridge and Clothier were built on Market Street.

Philadelphia was changing, as was every other city in the United States. Immigrants were streaming into the city. They were moving into row houses, crowded alleyways and boarding houses. Some became successful and began to move into more respectable areas.

The more established and affluent families then moved into the suburbs in order to live further away from the immigrants. Commuting became easy due to newly constructed railroads.

Morris and Molly

Chapter Eight

Real Estate

As newlyweds, Mollie and I had a wonderful life. My beautiful Mollie was the joy of my life, but very innocent in the ways of the world. I found myself straying from time to time with women who offered me more excitement. I still struggled to find a career. I sold automobiles and was one of the first to own one in Philadelphia, but I had this burning desire to do something more interesting, not only for the money but because I had the need to be successful.

One day, I went to my favorite barber shop for a shave and a haircut. As I waited my turn, I noticed a nice-looking young man in the barber's chair. He was about my age with black hair and sparkling dark brown eyes. He was telling the barber that he had just opened a real estate office around the corner, off Chestnut Street. I was more than intrigued and sat there trying to listen. I heard him say, "There is a great opportunity for real estate in Philadelphia, and I am just beginning to develop some properties."

When I finally sat in the chair, I asked the barber about him. His name was David Green. He was an immigrant from the Ukraine. That's all he knew, but that was enough.

I found his name and the real estate office on a small narrow street off Chestnut Street and went there right from the barber shop. There was a single desk where an attractive secretary greeted me. A typewriter was on the desk with a used file cabinet next to it. There was a large, comfortable leather chair and a wooden chair with slats, all used but in good taste, and a standing lamp with Tiffany glass. I waited a little while, was shown into Mr. Green's office and inquired about working there.

He sat behind a large mahogany desk with an American flag behind him. He was tall with dark hair, neatly cut. I was glad to be able to say I had experience and had worked for the firm Baker, Ingham and Hewitt. David and I quickly became friends when we discovered we had both come from Russia. We found we had so much in common. He had just started the company and was operating on a shoestring.

David was also very smart. He had a skill for reading people. He could get them to do what he wanted through charm or strong persuasion. He had an excellent memory and remembered every small detail, which allowed him to merge real estate development and finance. There was never an investment he did not like, from just selling houses to hotels to developing properties. Like me, he was very interested in being an American.

I learned from him. The company grew quickly, and the staff increased, making it an important company. He and I worked hand in hand, and I soon earned his confidence. He made me Vice President.

There was a lot of land to be bought and sold in Philadelphia in those formative years. We became important deal makers. In 1918 David formed the Bankers Security Corporation for general investment banking. It handled virtually all his financial interests, but a run on the bank ended his career as a banker, leaving him millions in debt.

Our small company had grown to be one of the largest in the country, but, as the owner, David had to resign to pay his debts. I remained in charge and took over. Our company flourished. We built famous department stores and hotels. I became one of the wealthiest men in Philadelphia. It was the American dream.

Life was good. Molly had blessed me with a daughter and four sons. I made sure my children had an education. We had a good family, and they grew quickly.

My daughter Cecelia was still very young when she met Herman at a Halloween party.

Herman Mark Watkins came to America from Russia with his mother, brothers and sisters when he was very young. His father died shortly after their arrival here, leaving the young widow to raise their five children.

Herman had to work selling anything he could. The family struggled just to put food on the table. It was too close to my own story. I had hoped Ceal would marry a doctor or lawyer and a real American.

Herman was good looking and spoke with a very slight accent, which only added to his charm. Even though I did not approve, I could see that they were very much in love.

When they married, I took Herman into the company with me. He was a quick learner. Later he took law courses, but never graduated.

I had a secretary by the name of Rose. She was sharp as well as young and sexy. One day she stayed late to finish typing some letters. It was well after 5 o'clock, and everyone had left for the day. She always seemed interested in the company and asked me some questions.

As she handed me the letters, she brushed up against me. It was obviously on purpose. Her body was young and supple. I led her to the leather sofa. We kissed as I felt the warmth of her thighs and stroked her lightly under her panties. I cupped her ample breasts in my hands and gently nudged her legs apart. She seemed to enjoy it as much as I did as we had a lingering kiss.

I knew I was attractive to women but was angry at myself for losing control. It was not smart to mix business and pleasure. I decided to reassign her to Herman, my son-in-law, to avoid further temptation. I should have known better, but I was too impressed with my own virility to realize what I had done.

There was rent to be collected. The firm had recently built an impressive office building with some important tenants. Rose took over this job. She also lined up investors for Herman to meet, and they began traveling together. My daughter Ceal became concerned and talked to me about it, but they seemed to have a happy marriage, so maybe it was only business. She confided in me that she and Herman were trying to have a baby.

Ceal and Herman seemed happily married. They both liked

music. I had given them a baby grand piano when they moved into their new house. The house had just been built, and they were the first to live in it. Ceal loved to cook for him. They often invited friends for dinner.

Herman loved Enrico Caruso, the famous Italian street singer, and Ceal played all the popular tunes on the piano. They often went to Atlantic City and met with Herman's brother Mark and his wife Esther. They swam in the ocean, and the men played ball on the beach. Many evenings they sat out under the stars at Robin Hood Dell listening to the outdoor concerts. To a casual observer they had an idyllic life.

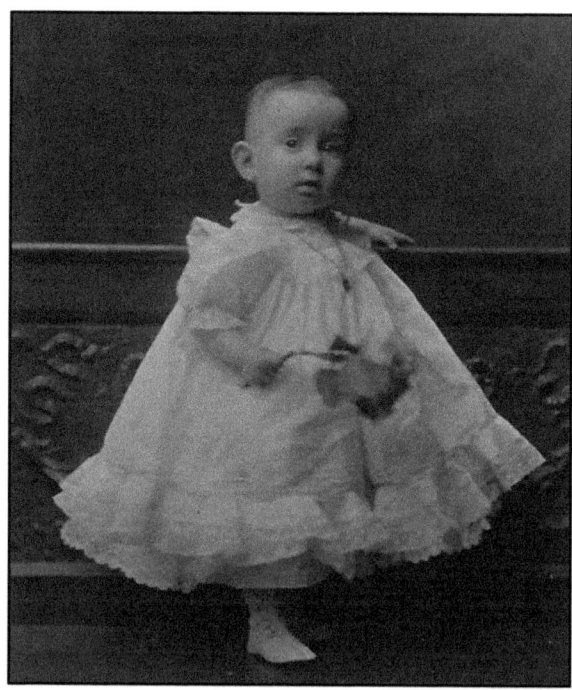

Cecelia

Chapter Nine

Marcy is Born
1925

Ceal became pregnant, and I felt, with this joy in their lives, Herman would give up his affair with Rose.

Rose would often leave something in his suitcase when he returned home from a week-end to let Ceal know that they had been together. Though she became suspicious, Ceal felt it not wise to accuse him of infidelity.

My daughter was an idealist. She believed in a fairy tale love. I could not remake her into a scheming, sensuous woman. She often stopped in the office and chatted with Gladys, who worked in the outer office to direct clients.

Everyone liked Ceal. There was something elegant about her with her dark hair and almond shaped eyes. People often described her as a lovely lady. And that she was.

Herman held an important position in the firm. He was very good looking. He had a neatly trimmed moustache, sparkling brown eyes and a confident, outgoing personality.

I decided to talk to Herman man to man. He assured me that he and Ceal had a happy marriage and that Rose meant nothing to him. He was convincing and offered to swear on his father's grave.

Ceal was so happy and grew big with child. Herman was home every night and seemed devoted to her. There were no more weekends to visit investors. But Rose was clever and even turned him against Ceal, so that when Marcy was born, he was not even at the hospital.

Herman fell in love with his baby daughter and moved back to his little family. He was a proud daddy at his little girl's first birthday party. The little boy from next door was there and a few other children from the neighborhood. Marcy had a big bow in her hair. Herman held Ceal's hand as he helped blow out the one candle on the birthday cake.

Through the business, Rose found ways to control his life again. Meanwhile, with investors and bank loans, our firm was building hotels and important landmarks in Philadelphia. We were successful beyond my dreams, and I was always able to pay off our loans. As president of the company, I signed for these loans, and my credit was impeccable—until 1930 when the depression hit! Real estate was hit hard. There was a run on the banks and every bank called in its loans. I was wiped out like everyone else, except for Herman, who made a profit but never signed anything.

Ceal and daughter Marcy at Marcy's Birthday Party

He and Rose planned on leaving the company and were stashing their money away to be able to make a fresh start. He was now able to buy properties for nothing and to benefit from the losses. Rose was like his partner, and I could see her clever maneuvering behind his business success.

He seldom came back home and even refused to support Ceal and Marcy. Ceal had to give up their house to move in with Mollie and me. Fortunately, we had a big house and still had our sons Danny, Leonard, and Arthur living there. We also had Mollie's mother living with us, as she needed help in her elder years. Our oldest son, Harry, had a law practice and was able to support himself.

Herman asked Ceal for a divorce.

Every weekend he picked up Marcy and took her somewhere special. Sometimes on Sundays he took her out horseback riding. She loved Brownie. He was like an overgrown pony and very tame. Herman bought Marcy a tricycle and taught her how to ride it.

Her favorite treat was when they went to the whispering wall in Fairmont Park. He would whisper on one end of the wall, and then she would answer on the other end. Her sweet little voice carried like an echo, "I love you, Daddy."

In the fall the leaves would be red and gold, and the forest would surround them with the clean, pungent smell of pine. On the way home, the car radio was tuned to the vibrant voice of Caruso. Herman would pull up to the house and watch as Marcy walked up the steps to the front door.

Once she was inside, Ceal held her tight to smell the lingering aroma of Herman's cigar. Marcy was bubbling over to tell her mother about her day with Daddy and all about the whispering wall.

Her uncles wanted to hear, too. Before long, Mommy was playing the piano, and they were all singing. At dinner, everything was passed around the table while the best was saved for Marcy. She always wanted to sit next to her Uncle Danny, who was her favorite. He read the funny papers to her every Sunday morning. Her Grandma Molly sat at one end of the big table, and I at the other.

During the daytime, Mollie sat at the table and put eyelets in the labels on small cellophane bags full of chocolate covered nuts and raisins. The labels read Silver Candy Company. She had a special machine for this. You could hear the rhythmic *click click* as she worked. She then hung the bags on a metal tree, and I took them to sell at drug stores and candy stores.

I worked downstairs in the large basement, where I had a big vat of melting chocolate into which I dipped the nuts and raisins. I also made "Marcy Mae Puffs," which turned out to be a huge success. My customers kept ordering large quantities of these candy bars. During the depression, it was a living.

One crisp autumn day when Marcy went out with Herman, she came home with a pink satin ballet dress with a net skirt sprinkled with gold stars. She said that "the nice lady made it for her for Halloween." She did not understand what she had said to make her mommy cry.

Ceal tried to explain to Marcy that Rose was not a nice lady and that "She had taken her daddy away from us." The next time Rose was with them, Marcy told Rose, "My mommy says you are a bad lady." When they went to see the stage show at the movie house, Marcy tried not to sit next to Rose. She felt she was being disloyal to her mother.

Ceal had become painfully thin. She was so thin that her bones stuck out. One day, she lay on the sofa in the living room, and Mollie hovered over her. She looked as though she would have welcomed death and was that still. I heard Mollie say, "Ceal, you must live for Marcy." I saw Marcy looking down through the railing, watching. She looked frightened. It was the day that the divorce became final.

The next day, Herman and Rose were married.

Part II

Marcy

Chapter Ten

My Grandparent's House

Mother and I moved into my grandparent's house. I was just starting kindergarten, and every morning my grandfather drove me to the Bryant School. He would give me five shiny pennies. He said they had just come from the Mint. He was devoted to me and was an important part of my life.

Mother left for work selling clothes at Blauner's Department Store and came home very tired, but the sight of me seemed to cheer her up. I tried to do small things to make her smile. She and I were friends, and she shared everything with me, even as a little girl. In some way, I felt the need to take care of my mother. I knew she was unhappy, and I knew she missed my daddy. She used to tell me that I must always love him.

Mother and I shared the back bedroom that looked over the small garden. I loved to sit on the window seat and watch the taffy colored cat playing in the alley. My favorite toy was a big brown monkey I called Shnokelpuss. He sat on my bed.

When I came back from a visit with my father, I saw my mother waiting for me at the front door. I was glad to be back home with my three uncles who were more like big brothers to me. Every Saturday Arthur (we called him Otzy) would take me to the Crosskeys to see a movie. That's when I started to collect stamps, as they gave out packets of stamps. Otzy was the youngest of my uncles.

I liked living at my grandparents, but I still remember Otzy telling me that this was not my home and that nobody wanted me. My Uncle

Danny sometimes took me with him when he went out on dates. I liked his girlfriend, Esther.

I often walked down to the corner to the Acme to buy groceries for my grandma. A loaf of bread cost seven cents.

We had a black maid. Her name was Marie. I really liked Marie. She told me "how babies are made" in great and too graphic detail. She was very helpful to my grandmother.

My grandfather always sat behind the large roll-top desk with the wall phone within his reach. He told me that when he was younger, he had the first automobile in Philadelphia.

His dark hair had some gray in it now. His mustache was always neatly trimmed, and he wore glasses to read. He always smoked cigarettes, right to the very end. To the child that was me, he was perfect and could do no wrong.

We would sit around the cabinet-sized radio as we listened to President Roosevelt. He always started his Fireside Chat with, "My fr-i-e-n-d-s." He gave the country hope.

I loved to watch my grandmother sitting at her dressing table, brushing her long hair and then piling it up into a knot at the nape of her long neck. Her skin was like marble, and she always smelled like fresh flowers.

She had brown eyes and was always calm and serene. She told me many times, "Be nice to everyone, and everyone will be nice to you."

My great grandmother had the room next to the bathroom. She was very old and frail and hunched over. She sat on the glassed-in front porch and rocked in her rocking chair. When I was little, she used to want to hide me when the lady with the big eyes came to call, as she said the lady had "the evil eye." She also said that I was born with a "lucky veil."

I loved to sit with her and listen to her stories. She told me that she had once gone to a wedding in the "old country" and that the earth opened up and swallowed the bride and groom. She told me that when she married my great grandfather, the first time she saw him was when he lifted the veil at their wedding. She said that God had a big golden book and everything that would happen to me in my life was written in that book.

I was old for my age and learned to be independent, but no matter what games I played with friends or what schoolwork I had or what was happening at home, my first priority was to see my Daddy.

Chapter Eleven

Daddy's House

It was chilly as I waited for the bus that Friday. I was glad I had thought to grab my coat at the last minute. I wore the black and white checked skirt and starched white blouse mother had put out for me. I remembered to take my gloves, and I swung my pocketbook on my arm.

It was the same bus driver as always. "Packard Building?" he asked. "Yes, thank you," I replied, choosing the empty seat opposite him. I was happy to be able to go by myself to see my Daddy.

As we traveled the familiar route, I was looking forward to the time I would spend alone with Daddy. I often had a picture in my mind of that little girl running down to the corner every night to wait for him when he came home from work and chatter on about my day. I always saw him looking at me with that wonderful smile. Then the small voice inside of me scolded, *"Stop looking back! I did feel sorry for myself. Stop that too!"*

I wondered about what my great grandmother told me. She was so old and so wise. Was there really such a thing as God's big golden book? I even wondered about God and how He could have allowed Rose to come into our lives.

I thought about Elsie Dinsmore in the book I was reading and how her faith kept her strong. She was my role model, so I had to believe. I had heard bits and pieces of things that children should not know— not that I understood it all. But I understood enough to know that Rose had taken my Daddy away from us.

Somehow, I seemed to know as a little girl that when Rose said hurtful things to me, it was better not to answer her. I even knew enough to pity her for her hateful thoughts. I had learned then to remain calm and even sorry for her unhappiness. I felt sorry for my mother, too. She loved my father so much.

Tomorrow would be my tenth birthday, and I was hoping that maybe Daddy would take me to see the dancing girls tonight. Rose would probably come, too. With it all, I sometimes liked Rose. That would make me feel a little guilty. Then she would hurt my feelings again and make me want to cry, but I didn't!

As the bus came to a stop at the corner of the busy intersection, the nice driver opened the door for me to get off. The policeman, who was always on that corner on Fridays, stopped traffic and walked across the street with me, right to the revolving door of the office building. I took the elevator to the 11th floor and walked into the suite of rooms, past many nods and welcoming smiles. Daddy was on the phone, so I went to wait for him where his secretary Gladys was sitting at the typewriter. I liked to watch her as she rhythmically hit every key without even looking. She always finished quickly when I was there and turned the typewriter over to me.

It was fun getting into Daddy's red roadster with the top down and driving to his house. It was good to be with him. I loved him so much and hoped he loved me, too.

The house was big, and when I walked into the large foyer with French doors framing the trees, now crowned with leaves of red and gold, Daddy would disappear up the winding staircase. I waited dutifully in the large green leather chair studded with brass nail heads. I felt the hush of respectful silence. When he and Rose walked down from the bedroom together, Daddy was no longer in his impeccable navy suit. He had changed to his baggy old trousers, a frayed shirt and a hat that had long ago lost its shape. Before the sun went down, he needed to tend to his roses.

Rose gave me a small peck on the cheek. "Would you like to see your baby sister?" she asked as she led me upstairs to the nursery. The baby was so tiny and sweet. I longed to touch her little fingers, but Rose cautioned me not to get too close, as I should not breathe my germs on her.

The bell rang, calling us to the dinner table. The dining room was off the foyer with two doors opening onto the terrace. On warm evenings, we sometimes ate out there under the green and white awning. I liked that, as it was not as formal. Clarence, in his white jacket, passed each platter, and I lifted the food onto my plate as I was taught. I was careful to break the roll into small pieces from the bread and butter plate. It sure wasn't like the meals at my grandparents, where my uncles reached across the table.

It was mostly grown-up talk, so I only half listened, but I certainly perked up on this night when Rose told me that after dinner, we would go to the Fox to see the stage show. The meal seemed to drag on. Finally, we were at the front door as I slipped into my coat.

Rose looked at me disapprovingly. "You mean you did not wear your good coat?" she asked.

"No." I hung my head, thinking, "How stupid of me."

"Well, I'm sorry; we cannot take you to the Fox looking like that. Maybe this will teach you a lesson, and you will pay attention to how you dress after this." She took off her coat and went upstairs.

Daddy looked at me with pity. I wasn't sure what kind of pity it was, whether he was sad for me or thought, too, that I was pretty dumb. He never said, but when he drove me home to my grandparent's house, he was very quiet. As he opened the door for me to get out, he handed me an envelope and said, "Give this to your Mommy and tell her to buy you something special for your birthday." He gave me a big hug as he kissed me goodnight.

Marcy Riding at Wissahicken Park

Chapter Twelve

Summer Camp

My dad came to camp every Fourth of July with an exciting show of fireworks that he set off in a boat on the camp lake. I went to camp every summer until I was about 15 years old.

Sometimes on Sunday morning, Dad would take me horseback riding at Wissahicken Park. We would tie up the horses and go to the Inn for bacon and eggs. Rose had trouble handling the horse, as much as she tried.

I went to Miss Cherry's dancing class, where I took ballet and tap lessons. I was so excited to be in our dance recital. My costumes were just gorgeous. My ballet outfit was all pink with a lovely net skirt. The music was from "The Nutcracker Suite." My tap-dancing costume was royal blue shiny satin shorts with a matching top and full red see-through gauze sleeves and a royal blue top hat. Could you believe it? At the last minute, I got chicken pox and could not be in the show.

I walked to the Bryant School. At recess I could buy a flavored water ice, or sometimes I would buy a piece of chocolate candy. If the inside turned out to be pink, I could get another one free.

After school I would go around the corner to roller skate with Janie. Janie was very pretty, and when we would play with the boys, they always tried to catch her, but not me. Sometimes we would chalk a grid on the sidewalk and play hopscotch.

I would always end the day by walking to the elevator on Market Street to meet mother coming home from work. We would hold hands on the way home, and I would then rub her tired feet in a basin of warm water.

"Did a lot of ladies come to buy dresses today?" I would ask. There was always a story. Mother loved to tell me stories.

She used to tell me what a beautiful baby I was and how she liked to take me on the trolley car because people would make a fuss over me.

Mother told me that once when we were on the trolley car, we passed a church with a revolving cross and underneath it said, "God is Love." She always told me that nothing was more important in life than love. She would say that millionaires couldn't buy it.

Sometimes on a Saturday, Mother and I would go to the Chinese restaurant called Cathay on Chestnut Street. A fortune teller there read my tea leaves. She said that I would travel over many oceans. We thought that was very funny.

On weekends, Uncle Mike, Mother's friend, would take us for a ride in the country. Uncle Mike was a doctor.

"When we are married," he'd say to Mother, "You can help me with patients." He told Mother that he would be sure she dressed stylishly because people would say, "The doctor must be doing well. Look at the expensive clothes his wife wears."

He always had a new book he wanted Mother to read, and, even if the sun was out, he carried an umbrella. Once he took me to see a field of daisies and let me pick a big bunch to take home. I wish mother had married him instead of Uncle Lou.

At least mother did not have to work anymore. She and Uncle Lou moved to the Cobb's Creek Apartments, and I would visit with her after school until Uncle Lou came home. It was about five blocks to my grandparent's house.

One rainy, windy day, I was feeling sick. My head hurt and my throat was sore, but I knew I had to leave before Lou came home. I guess he just didn't like children.

"You lie here on the sofa," Mother said. "You cannot go out in this downpour."

When Uncle Lou came home, I heard him say, "Marcy must live with us now." I felt hot and cold. Mother put a blanket over me, and I fell asleep, but I heard them talking over dinner. Lou had a friend who was a lawyer. They decided to take my father to court for more money so I could live with them.

During the court hearing, the judge ordered more child support and also that a psychiatrist talk to me. The doctor advised that I was in an unhealthy atmosphere and that it would be harmful for me to continue to feel a split loyalty to both of my parents. I think that was when my father decided to send me to boarding school.

I went to camp every summer until I was in my teens. I was a senior. One day I was in the shower and singing to myself but loud enough to be heard. Herb Dorshow, who was a counselor at camp, heard me singing and asked me to try out for the camp play. He was the director of the show. He had a wonderful voice and was very good looking. I did get the leading part in the musical "Good News," and Herb and I became very close, even through my years at college.

Herb was my first real boyfriend. Even though he was a lot older than I, our relationship lasted many years. He was studying medicine at Jefferson Hospital, and at one point, he gave me his Phi Beta Kappa key (an honor given for excellence in academics). It was expected that we would be married.

When I was about seventeen, I went to Palm Beach at Christmas break from school to be with my father and Rose. We would stay at the Palm Beach Hotel, and Herb would come too.

Rose arranged for us to have adjoining rooms. Even though Herb was certainly romantic and, when we were in each other's arms, nothing in the world mattered, we did not make love. I was determined that would never happen until I was married.

Rose would often give me little "gems" of advice as I became a teenager. One of her favorites was, "A smart woman will use her body to get what she wants."

Herb did not come from a prestigious family, and Rose would call him a "beggar on horseback." She told me that he was only interested in my father's money.

My father belonged to a prestigious beach club where he and Rose had a large and comfortable cabana. I loved to swim in the ocean and would swim far out. I loved water skiing and was good at diving in the pool. Sometimes on a date, Herb and I would go there to neck.

A few years later, we spent Christmas at the Whitehall Hotel, which had originally been the Flagler Mansion, and Herb was invited to come too. By then Susie was born, and the children were there with Mademoiselle, their nanny. I liked her very much, and I also loved my little sisters.

Later, my father bought a magnificent house on Lake Worth, and I continued to visit him there "during season."

When I was ready to go to junior high school, I was sent to Edgewood Park in Scarborough, New York, on the Hudson. It was more of a finishing school than for academics. It had a large sprawling campus and was formerly a resort for gentlemen and their "lady friends."

The school suggested that I travel with another student from Philadelphia. We were to leave by train on Sunday morning. I was supposed to meet Bonnie Smythe at the 30th street station at 10 a.m. Her mother called my mother that Sunday morning to arrange to take a later train. She said that Bonnie had had a late night and had a little hangover. Bonnie was entering junior college.

She was there waiting for me as I arrived at the station. She was surrounded by all sizes of leather and alligator-trimmed suitcases. She was wearing a green velvet suit with a matching hat and high spiked heels. She was quite sophisticated, and I felt somewhat dowdy in my plain camel hair blazer, skirt and sweater with saddle shoes.

When I left my mother, even though I was excited, I could see how unhappy she was that I was leaving.

At school, as one approached through the imposing front door, there sat one of the staff at the "social desk" where dates were made at West Point and the neighboring Peekskill Academy for Boys, mostly at the request of a girl's mother.

The first day I was there, I was assigned a room and a roommate, who was in junior college. Her name was Elsie Abotball, and we became close friends. Elsie's parents lived in South America, where she was born. I loved her Spanish accent and the way she pronounced my name: "Maaarcy."

We had a large dorm room on the second floor. Chapel was obligatory, and it was where I first learned *The Lord's Prayer*.

On one occasion, I stopped in to see Bonnie. She showed me her different-sized perfume bottles containing scotch, bourbon and gin.

She told us about how she climbed out the window and went into town. We all listened breathlessly as she talked about the men she picked up and her sexual encounters.

Elsie and I remained best friends all through school. She was my only friend. I learned in those years to hold my head high and to walk with confidence. Inside, though, I still felt like the little girl who did not deserve to occupy space in the world.

Summers, when I was home from school, I worked at the newspaper as a copy girl. My father was upset that I did not ask him about working there, as he would have spoken to his friend, Walter Annenberg, who owned the paper, and gotten me a better job, at least with better hours. I had fun working there and felt I wanted to study journalism in college.

When we graduated, Elsie returned to Columbia. I never saw or heard from her again, though I tried to find an address.

Herb was still in my life and was now like "part of the family," but Mother did not feel he was right for me. He had to do his residency in South Dakota, so for some time we did not see much of each other but were always in touch.

I had applied to college, and though I wanted to go to Cornell, I was not accepted. My father said, "You're not going to let that stop you, are you? Why don't you get on the train and go to Cornell?" And so that was what I did. The Dean said they would take me in Home Economics but not Liberal Arts. My father then suggested that I go to Syracuse University. By then, I was tired and had caught a cold. I had a sore throat, a cough, and probably had a temperature. I sat in the Dean's office at Syracuse, waiting for him over an hour. When he finally arrived, I guess he could see that I was not very well and was compassionate. He said, "Can you start in two weeks?"

Marcy at Syracuse University
Class of 1947

Chapter Thirteen

Syracuse University

So there I was in the summer session at Syracuse University. It was that summer that I discovered a real social life. The ASTP and the Air Corp were stationed at Syracuse. We were in World War II. The boys would march in formation on campus, singing, "The girl on the right is plenty alright, *parlez vous?* Does the girl on the right have a date tonight, *parlez vous?*" I became popular and had dates but mostly with the servicemen. Maybe I was not so ugly as Rose said I was.

There were not so many men students at school those years because of the war. I did not join a sorority. I could not rush that first year as I had received a D in Political Science. Many of the fraternity boys only dated girls from sororities, so I was not in the "in" crowd. I guess I never have been, nor have I wanted to be. The boys I dated in those years went off to war, and some of them never came back. Herb came to see me often at school and was ready to become a specialist in urology. We were growing apart.

Once I was on the train on my way home and a few of the GI's tried to get fresh with me. A young soldier came to my rescue. He stepped up and said, "You are talking to my wife." I had no more trouble and ended up sitting with him. His name was Clarence Otha Paugh, and he and I then saw a lot of each other until he had to leave for the front.

My mother loved me so and told me if I walked erect and believed I was beautiful, I would be beautiful. Many times in my life, I felt very small and had to remember her words. Without her great love for me and her great confidence in me, I would not have been able to hold my head up high during the rough times in my life.

She had a recurring dream about me—that I was in danger. She could not find me but finally did. I was hiding in a church.

From the time I was a little girl, she told me about the handsome prince. It never happened for her, although I knew she never stopped loving my father. But it did happen for me. I guess I will always believe in fairy tales.

I was happy at college, since I was not being torn between my mother and father. I liked being independent and making my own decisions. I found it amazing to see parents drive up with loaded cars to help students get settled in the dorms. Not once did anyone in my family come to see me. At least my mother and my grandmother came to my graduation at Edgewood Park.

It was very cold in Syracuse, and it seemed it was always snowing there. I learned to ski at Drumlins. Afterward, we sat around a large fireplace to get warm. A huge chandelier reflected colored prisms in the darkened room as we danced. It was so romantic.

I was a conscientious student and, after goofing off that summer, with my new-found freedom, I made the Dean's list every year and was accepted into the Psychology Honorary.

I did not stick around for graduation. I had something more important in my life now, as I married Martin Frank three weeks before graduation.

My relationship with Herb was over, mainly because he was not sensitive enough to my problems.

I met Martin through Marilyn Cantor. Marilyn was the daughter of Polly, who was Rose's best friend. I fell in love with Martin, and he was the answer to all my problems. He lived in New York City. He was rich, and I would not have to go back to Philadelphia. He was ten years older than I was and very sophisticated. He was right at home at The Stork Club and at "21."

It was an interesting arrangement that Rose had with Polly. Polly's husband owned a small department store in Potsdam, New York. Polly refused to live in the "sticks," especially because she didn't see how Marilyn would ever find a rich husband in a little hick town. Polly and Marilyn had a modest apartment. Polly made flowered hats, which were all the rage in those years. If one were to meet the mother and daughter, they would think that both had the manner of being born with a silver spoon.

Polly lived with my father and Rose, as it gave a prestigious address and phone number that Marilyn could use. It was not a spoken agreement, to my knowledge, but Polly was a role model for Rose, teaching her how to dress and how to entertain so that she could take her rightful place in society. Polly knew everyone who was anyone.

Marilyn was instructed to do the same for me. No matter how much time we spent together, we were never good friends. Still, Marilyn took her mission to remake me very seriously.

She said I walked with tiny steps. I was to take big steps. She also said I had terrible taste in clothes and was instructed to select my clothes for me. She said I had a big wide grin. When Marilyn said, "Laugh, clown, laugh," it was my signal to stop smiling.

Marilyn was about two years older than I was. She had dark hair and was sultry and sensuous looking. My father called her "velvet ass."

Marilyn became engaged to marry Stanley Ballin, who was Martin's business partner and friend. When Marilyn met Stanley, it was the "catch of the century." His company made woven automobile seat covers. Their office was at 630 Fifth Avenue near Rockefeller Plaza. Martin's family owned a paper mill in Gilman, Vermont. Gilman was the family name. Everyone who lived there worked for the company.

Marcy and her Step Sisters
at her Engagement Party

Chapter Fourteen

Martin

It turned out that Martin's family became mine, too. His mother, Celia Frank, became my dearest friend and remained so until she died, even though Martin and I were divorced after eight years.

It was understood that we would be married by a justice of the peace in Syracuse, as my father and Rose refused to be at a wedding if my mother was there. Even though Rose refused to be in the same room with my mother, she had a huge engagement party for me. She had long blue dresses made alike for my two stepsisters and me (a far cry from the white bridal dress that every girl dreams of wearing).

There was a live band, ice sculptures, incredible food, all under a huge tent. The guest list included all her friends, but no family. Of course, Martin's family and friends were invited and a few friends of mine.

I can still see Martin in his tuxedo, looking very handsome and debonair. He looked like he belonged in a tuxedo. He had a swarthy oriental look about him. His slanted dark eyes were quizzical, and he always seemed to be in control of every situation. I was twenty-one and he was thirty-one. I learned later that he had been married before.

There was another side to Martin that I fell in love with. He could suddenly become a little boy, sweet, winning, someone to whom you could deny nothing.

At times he was warm, gentle and loving. He would say as we walked into a restaurant, "Just watch, every head will turn to look at you and wonder how I ended up with someone so beautiful."

61

Then there were times that I would seek out his hand and he would quickly pull it away, as though to touch me would contaminate him.

We were a beautiful couple. He was dashing and charming and sensuous looking. When we did the tango, the floor cleared to watch us. We were in perfect step.

However, the engagement party was a sham. It was a far cry from every girl's dream of walking down the aisle with an adoring father at her side. My darling mother-in-law, who remained my best friend for life, saw through all the icing and was determined to make it up to me. That she did! She showered me with lovely gifts and with true affection. She bought me a beautiful trousseau.

Rose found herself on a social level that was new to her. Celia was a graduate of the finest schools and comfortable with people who were names out of the society column. She loved me dearly, as I did her, and always introduced me as "her little daughter." Through the years, there was nothing we did not share and no secrets between us. Rose held her in awe and did not dare to cross her.

My father arranged for us to have the bridal suite at the elegant Flagler Mansion in Palm Beach on our wedding night. It was very romantic as we climbed the marble steps up to the glamorous bedroom, but our first night together was not what a young virgin would expect, as Martin was unable to consummate our marriage.

In our marriage, I longed for a warmth he never gave, and often wondered if he had it to give, not to me,

Marcy on her Honeymoon

but only to other women. I did learn ways to arouse him, but we did not have sex often. Still, we had two beautiful baby boys.

We had an apartment on 75th and Madison Avenue with just a short walk to Central Park. I used to love to wheel David there in his English baby pram.

We were invited to dinner parties and were booked weeks in advance. We met friends and entertained at the famous Stork Club and "21."

We were wildly popular and, although Martin did not make that much money, his mother subsidized our extravagant life style.

Marilyn settled down with Stanley, and we spent a great deal of time together. I liked Stanley. Though they were always having gourmet dinner parties, Stanley was not a big spender. Marilyn spent her time shopping at Bonwits and Bergdorf Goodman.

She liked me to go shopping with her, as Stanley seemed to trust me, and I would always come to her defense. She would often overspend.

On one of these days, as we lunched at Schraffts, Marilyn told me in confidence about a scene overheard by her mother Polly. My father and Rose were having an argument about me. Rose was trying to convince my father to cut me out of his will. "Hermsky," she said, using her affectionate nickname for my father, "She is not our flesh and blood. You do enough for her."

Marilyn was trying to warn me, and with good cause, but throughout my life I believed in my father's sense of fairness. Martin and I confronted them with the information, which they denied.

After that, Marilyn was no longer in Rose's favor. I did not realize that this was to be a lifelong ambition for Rose. She once said to me, "I will get my revenge on you, if I have to come back from the grave to do it." For what? I did not understand.

Another time, at lunch in New York, she told me, "I will see that your father takes care of you if you always look after your two sisters." I did not have a real relationship with Jackie but felt closer to Susie. When there were family plans, I was pretty much left out. I remember once when a photographer was there to take a family picture, Rose told me I was not to be in it as I was not a member of the family.

I once went to the hairdresser with Rose. She was given a smock to change into as was customary at this upscale beauty parlor. Rose insisted on wearing no cover over her black "merry widow" corset. She said it cost a lot of money and she refused to wear anything over it.

After Marilyn and Stanley were married several years, Marilyn confided in me that she was having an affair with a married man. She was totally infatuated with him and would meet him afternoons and tell Stanley that she was shopping with me. After her rendezvous, she would meet me and describe in great detail their sexual activity. Together we would return to her apartment.

One day, Stanley was waiting at the door and told her she was not to come in, that he would send her belongings to her and arrange for a divorce. He must have been suspicious and had her followed by a detective. Even though I never thought of her as a good friend, I did go with her to Alabama to get a divorce. I would not desert her when she was in trouble.

Celia and Ben spent their summers in the family home in Gilman, Vermont. It was a large, roomy, but modest house with a sloping green front lawn. I always spent the months of July and August with them. Martin would come for long weekends. Martin, Howard and I would swim at the lake and I would water ski on the back of the motor boat.

Sylvia and Charlie, Martin's aunt and uncle, had a sprawling home that they built in the mountains that overlooked the whole valley. It was called Panorama Farms. Martin's cousin Howard had a stable of working stock horses. The three of us would go to the Lancaster Fair to show the horses. My favorite was a beautiful Palomino called Amber. She was so smart; she could turn on the radio. In the middle of the night, music would come from the barn.

On Saturday nights, Martin and I would dress and go to the Mt. Washington Hotel dances. We would meet new friends who we would invite to the lake for a barbecue. Those were idyllic days, and I loved my new family, who embraced me as their own.

Martin and I decided to move to the suburbs. My father had a custom designed house built for us in Hartsdale, New York, adjacent to a golf course. It was a modern ranch, all on one floor and beautifully designed. In the living room there were sliding glass windows and a field stone fire place that went from floor to ceiling and extended out to the adjoining terrace. All you could see was the green of the golf course.

Celia was a decorator and saw that it was beautifully furnished. She often took me with her when she went to wholesale fabric stores and furniture shops. I loved being with her and learned so much. She bought us the finest antiques. My father at the time owned the Warwick Hotel in Philadelphia, and he was able to order expensive linens wholesale for us.

I wanted very much for our marriage to work, but, as the years went on, Martin would leave me at parties and go off with someone else. Frequently his affairs would be with one of our friends. I felt it was my fault. At one time, my father came to see me and told me he wanted me to leave Martin because he was not faithful to me. I became angry at my father.

On New Year's Eve we arranged to have a weekend house party at Gilman, Vermont. We all took an overnight train. There was another couple, one of Martin's friends—more his age than mine. Helen Foster was with us, and her husband Malcolm was coming up the next day. Howard was there. I was aware that Howard was gay. He was my dearest friend and very protective of me. That night on the train, we drank a lot, and I realized that Martin kept filling my glass. I was suspicious, pretended to be drunk and crawled into my berth. After a while when all I could hear was the sound of the moving train, I went to Martin's berth and found him together with Helen.

There were excuses and protests. The picture that remains with me all this time is standing in the space between the cars and watching the tracks. Howard came to find me, and I cried as he tried to comfort me. I always forgave Martin and tried repeatedly until I felt so betrayed that I could no longer bear to be with him. He then had an affair with Miriam Freund, and when I came home one day, pregnant with Bob, I found them together.

Chapter Fifteen

Divorce

On our eighth wedding anniversary, we had dinner with Miriam and Jack Freund. I presented Martin with a gift of a divorce. He seemed genuinely upset, and at another time he could have convinced me that I was mistaken and that he really did love me—but I was hardened now and no longer susceptible to his lies

When I met next time with Celia and Ben, they treated me like a stranger. They had been told that I was having an affair with another man. Martin accused me of being unfaithful to him, and they believed him.

I moved to Upsal Gardens in Philadelphia. David was four and Bob was a year and a half. Mother and Lou lived in an apartment house around the corner from me. Martin did not have any intention of supporting us. He said my father was rich and could take care of us. He threatened to send information to the "Philadelphia Inquirer" to destroy my reputation.

My father asked me if anything Martin accused me of was true. I answered, "No."

"Even so," my father said, "let him keep his dirty moncy. We don't need it."

When I could I took the boys to see Celia and Ben in New York. They were always doting grandparents to the children.

Martin came to see the children about once a month and would take them for a ride and bring them home. We were not yet divorced but had a legal separation. Martin was living with Miriam, who left her husband and her four children.

One Christmas, when Martin came to visit, we went as a family to pick out a Christmas tree. It was a brief reconciliation.

I later found that the U.S. bonds that had been gifted to the children by their grandparents were missing. Martin claimed that he knew nothing about it and swore he had not taken them. I sent to the government for a copy. They were endorsed in my name but were signed in his handwriting.

Lou, who had always been so unaccepting of me, now loved David and Bob very much. He constantly reminded them that they were the "loves of his life." From the difficult man I had known since I was thirteen, when he married my mother, he now turned into a big gruff old teddy bear. I chastised myself that I had never taken the time to find that dear side of him. He never told me he loved me, but when the day came for me to move from my home in Hartsdale to my new apartment in Philadelphia, it was he who drove me and helped me move. It took until two the next morning.

Sad to say, I was so involved in my own life, that I did not visit my dearest grandfather, but he did see David when he was born and called him "King David."

My beautiful grandmother died at age 65 from an amputation caused by diabetes, and my grandfather, without his Mollie, lost his zest for living. For a while, he lived with Otzy and his wife Edythe, but he was not happy living there and went to live in a hotel for older gentlemen.

He only existed then. The man I felt could conquer the world had no will to live. He died at 86, probably from a broken heart.

My father was wonderful. He supported us. He paid the rent. He paid for private school for the boys. He bought me a beautiful white convertible.

I had a live-in maid named Josephine who helped with the children. I felt close to Josephine and urged her to go to school to better herself. It was not easy for black people in those years. Josephine married a young man by the name of David. I missed her when she left but found out years later that she did go to school and became a doctor. We are still good friends, and I am very proud of her.

I spent many weekends at my father's house, although neither he nor Rose ever gave the children much affection. One weekend when David visited them, Rose accused him of smoking a cigarette. She made quite a scene about it, and David was never invited back, nor did he want to go.

Rose was able to create situations that caused anger and hurt feelings. Even when I was a child, she tried to bait me so that I would answer her back, like the time she said, "Your grandmother was a stupid fat cow." Actually, I felt sorry for her and never did stoop to her level.

In later years, she would involve my father, so that he was forced to prove his loyalty to her by taking her side against me. Time and time again, I would write pleading letters to him, which he never answered. But during the years I was separated and living in Philadelphia, Rose was generous and supportive. It was a strange twist to her personality that when I felt rejected and lost in the confusion of a failed marriage, she was able to reach out to me. She and Dad even had meetings with Mother and Lou, as the four of them united to come to my rescue.

I had men friends, but only as friends. I was not serious about any of them. I did not want to date or to go to parties, but Mother almost pushed me out the door. I was afraid to trust a man again and definitely never wanted to marry. So, I just had fun.

I discovered years later that Martin was paying Clarence (Dad's chauffeur) to report all my activities to him and who I was seeing. He also had Mary, who helped me with the children, on his payroll.

My father bought property in Palm Beach and built small vacation houses near County Road. He gave me one of the houses during season, and he and Rose took me to parties and social events with them. I went but not with enthusiasm.

The little house was charming, with a lovely yard for the boys to play in, and there were other children on the block. Dad and Rose had a house quite near, and we spent a lot of time together.

On one occasion, they insisted on taking me to a party at the famous Patio Restaurant. I met a friend of theirs, who was widowed. I knew nothing about Nate. It was obvious he was much older than I was. He took me home from the party and tried to make love to me. The next day and every day thereafter, I received white orchids.

I liked him but knew I could never be happily married. I had been too hurt. We dated for a while, and a few weeks later he proposed to me. He showed me pictures of his various homes in Paris and Italy and of his huge yacht. I found out that he owned Sara Lee. I felt that I could have security the rest of my life and a good life for my children. I told him that I would think about it and let him know, but only if he wanted to marry me while knowing that I was not in love with him.

Chapter Sixteen

Fate Intervened

On New Year's Eve, 1956, I was invited to a New Year's Eve party in New York by a couple I did not know well. I was dating Julian, who came from Detroit and came often. He was serious about me but had been married four times. Though he was fun to be with and brought me lavish gifts, I kept telling him that I was not interested in getting married.

My mother had bought me a beautiful white lace dress with a sweetheart neckline. When we arrived at the party, their little girl answered the door and exclaimed, "Mommy, there is a fairy princess at the door."

I guess you might say that was a "grand entrance!" I met a couple there who asked me if I knew Henry Von Kohorn. I was not very interested in meeting anyone but gave them my phone number anyhow. A few weeks later Henry called me and asked me for a date. I told him I was leaving for Palm Beach if he would like to come there to meet me. He agreed, and we set a date.

I was still seeing Nate but had a date the day before with two nice guys who were just friends. We played tennis— if you want to call it that. It was the first time I ever held a racquet. We were really just fooling around on the court when I tripped on a tennis ball and sprained my ankle.

That evening, in my yellow polka dotted dress, with a ribbon around my hair and a bandage Dad put on my ankle, I met Henry at the tiny country airport in Palm Beach. In those days, you could walk right up to the gate to watch the plane land and to greet the passengers.

Henry, of course, asked me what I had done to my ankle. When I answered that I had sprained it playing tennis, he asked me if I liked tennis. I, of course, said, "Yes, I do," but did not tell him that I had never played before. He then asked me if I was good. I told him, "No, I'm not good," which could have been modesty on my part. Henry was an excellent player. He had a national ranking and played with some of the top players, but I did not know this when we met.

That evening was like fireworks! I knew at once he was everything I wanted in a man. Feelings long dormant were aroused in me. Driving in my open convertible to the Breakers Hotel, we hardly said a word to each other, but there was no need. There was magic between us.

When I waited for him in the lobby, I called my father on the pay phone to tell him that I just met the man I would marry. Dad asked me, "Does he know yet?" I answered, "No, but he will find out."

The next evening, when he picked me up at my father's house, I was still dressing, so Dad had a chance to meet him. He described the meeting to me later.

He offered Henry a drink and turned to make him a gin and tonic, then turned to make himself one. By then, Henry had finished his drink and requested another. Dad came upstairs to tell me that he thought my date had a hollow leg.

Today I laugh at that first meeting. Henry could really drink and never showed it. While I, on the other hand, could slide under the table with one martini.

We went dancing at the famous Taboo, and it was so right.

He told me about his wife, Joyce, who had died of polio two years earlier. I could feel his pain. He also told me how much he loved tennis.

Henry suggested that we go to Havana for the weekend, and I thought that was a great idea. We went to the airport to pick up tickets. When Henry asked for two round trip tickets, I said "No, I would have to have my sister come along." He had to ask for three tickets. In those days, Jackie and I were friends, and she was just "recovering" from a divorce, so she was happy to go. She was very obliging and left us alone.

I will never forget seeing Henry in a bathing suit with his

beautiful broad shoulders. Wow, was I smitten! Henry seemed to feel the same way, but, when you are young and in love, you don't always know if a man is sincere. I knew he had "designs" on me, but I guess he got the message that I was not "that kind of a girl."

Henry left Palm Beach to go on a business trip to Lima, Peru. I had invited him to come to my father's birthday party, but he said he could not come.

We had talked about going to Puerto Rico together, but I heard not a word and was miserable. I saw Nate meanwhile and confided in him that I had met someone and fallen in love. I knew now that I could not marry Nate who hoped I would change my mind.

Almost two weeks had gone by, and Mother called me frequently to come home. The maid had quit, and Mother was taking care of Bob and David. I tried to stay, hoping that I would just hear from Henry, but then gave up, as I knew I had to get back to my children. I had arranged to take an early flight from Palm Beach to Philadelphia. I'd given up hope of hearing from Henry.

It was seven-thirty in the morning, and I was getting ready to leave for the airport when the phone rang. "Hi, this is Henry. I'm at the airport. Can you come and get me?" I went to the airport, and the two of us took a plane back together, he to New York, and I to Philadelphia.

He came to see me the following weekend, and the weekend after that I went to New York to be with him. I stayed with Ralph, Henry's brother, and his wife, Dee, at their home in White Plains. Dee and I became best friends, and she told me that when Henry returned from having met me, he told Dee that he met someone special and that "she is a lady."

It was that weekend that I saw Henry Jr., Ken and Jeff playing baseball in the back yard at Bradford Road in Scarsdale. I loved them the minute I saw them, and my heart was broken for them, that they had no mother.

Henry had unexpected visitors, and he hustled me upstairs to avoid having to introduce me. I did not understand then, but knowing how private Henry was, I saw that he did not want anyone to know that there was someone he cared about.

Later Rose said to me that her friends were astounded that a mousy plain woman like Marcy could catch the most eligible bachelor in New York.

It was a whirlwind romance. Henry was honest, kind, loving and considerate. He treated me like a princess.

When my mother met him, she was horrified. She said he had holes on the bottom of his shoes and his shirt sleeves were frayed. She said I would have to go to work to support our five children and cautioned me to be careful. I saw none of this. I was so recklessly in love with him, I did not care.

When Henry came into my life, my whole world changed. All the years before, I had felt so insecure, trying to conform to people whose priorities were clothes, parties and gossip. I was no longer the ugly duckling with all the white swans. I had finally found my own kind.

One weekend when Henry came to Philadelphia, he stayed at 2601, an apartment hotel. He had reserved a bedroom and a living room. As always, I told him I would wait for him in the lobby, but this time he said, "I want you to come upstairs."

I protested, but he was very firm, so I did go upstairs with him. I sat on the sofa in the living room. He took his suitcase into the bedroom and came out with a magazine for me to read. It was "Business Week," and he pointed out Von Kohorn International Corporation on the cover of the magazine and the article inside. He was not wearing a shirt, and I could not concentrate. I just yearned to be in his arms.

I read the article but had no idea what I was reading. He came out again and kneeled before me. He said he wanted me to be his wife, but I did not need to answer him right away. It took me less than a second to say "Yes."

We had a brief engagement. We met in February, and we were married on April 2, 1956.

Henry took me to meet his mother in New York. He said, "I will leave you two ladies alone to get acquainted." His mother's first words to me were, "I never thought my son would marry a divorcee with two children." She next told me that she could never love any daughter-in-law as she had loved Henry's first wife Joyce. I guess I knew then that she and I would never be good friends, but I never gave up trying and always tried to be kind and attentive to her. She was my husband's mother. Who knows how I might have felt in her place?

The couple who introduced us was connected to Henry in business. He ran the Nylonge Plant which Henry owned. They were good friends and gave us a big engagement party at the Plaza Hotel.

Mother took me out shopping for a dress for that party. We bought a black taffeta dress that was cut to the waist in the back. It was a Christian Dior and had lovely lilacs at the back, three-quarter sleeves and boat neck. When Henry picked me up to go to the party, he said, "Whoever heard of flowers growing at your rear end," and insisted that I take off the lilacs. We both laughed. I should have known then.

Marcy and Henry on their Honeymoon

Chapter Seventeen

Marriage to Henry

I dreamed of having a wedding and being dressed as a bride, but Rose was not feeling well enough to arrange for an event, so we were married in St. Petersburg, Florida on April 2, 1956 by a Justice of the Peace. We had to be there to finalize my divorce, which I had never bothered to do in the year and a half in which I had a legal separation.

Our only witness was Henry Jr. Odessa, who was their housekeeper, was there and took little Henry home. We went to Jamaica to the Roundhill Resort for a glorious honeymoon. We were so much in love.

I guess the natural ending to this fairy tale romance would be that we lived happily ever after, and in a way we did. We had the ups and downs of most marriages, but we were in love "until death did us part."

I never knew I could be so happy. I was so in love with Henry, now and forever. Let me tell you about him.

His eyes were a grey-green but looked blue when he wore a blue shirt. He always had his eyeglasses and a pen in his shirt pocket. His hair was a sandy brown, but there wasn't much of it. Later, when he was older, he grew a bushy mustache, to protect his lip from the irritation of the sleep apnea device he had to wear. I trimmed it regularly to keep it tame.

When Henry had something funny to say, he would cock his head slightly, and there was a look, like a warning. His jokes were sometimes subtle, and you weren't sure what he meant. Sometimes, they were a little too naughty. Later in life when he spoke at family weddings, the new in-laws had to be warned. His jokes were often just plain silly, like the cannibal who was told to eat Aunt Milly. Strangers laughed to be polite.

He really didn't care what people thought of him, of what he wore or how he looked.

Henry's only act of vanity when he grew older was to keep that small strand of hair combed to the other side to hide his balding head. Of course, it never stayed there.

He was quiet. When other men were talking about their important business accomplishments or travel, he sat and listened. He had no need for one-upmanship or to impress anyone. The only bragging that got his attention were acts of heroism during the war. He was proud of his time in the service.

He loved music, especially Johann Strauss Jr. He read constantly and marveled at the miracles of the universe. He had a magnificent mind that often wandered into the abstract. He loved his six boys, the three he had with Joyce, who died, the two I had in an unhappy marriage, and the one we had together.

There was a kindness, a gentleness in his eyes, but when he was on the tennis court, he looked grim and determined.

When he held me in his arms, I fit perfectly into his shoulder, right above his heart. I wanted to bottle up those precious moments to pull out the cork when I missed him.

That summer, we rented a large house owned by Countess Morna in Scarsdale. We settled in with Odessa, Clifton, and the nurse who had been with the children, Emma. We also kept Juanita who had worked for me in Philadelphia.

One day I took Henry to the dentist, and he told me that Emma would kick him with her knee in the stomach. When we arrived home, I dismissed Emma.

Odessa had been with Henry and Joyce for many years. I felt the continuity was important for the children but, in her loyalty to Joyce, she resented me and refused to do anything for David and Bob. We had a split household, with Juanita cooking for one part of the family and Odessa for the other part. Since I knew that Henry and I would be looking for a home, I kept her and Clifton until we found our dream house in Greenwich, Connecticut. Once we moved in, I asked them to leave.

The one person who was truly magnificent was Joyce's mother. The first time I went to visit her in her sprawling, beautiful home in New Rochelle, with its manicured lawns and shrubs, I took all five of the boys. When we left, she lined them all up and gave each one of them a dollar. She said to David and Bob, "I always give my grandsons a dollar bill." She said to each, "Here is yours because now I am your Gaggy, too."

I marveled at her kindness to a woman who took her daughter's place. She was a warmhearted woman. I loved her at once and always. Her husband, Lou, was just as dear.

In the beginning, Henry, Ken and Jeff did not accept me. I could understand how hard it was for them and just continued to offer them love. It took a while until they knew they could trust me and that I wanted them to be as my own. One day, several months after we were in our home at Pecksland Road, I said something to Henry Jr. and he answered me back, "Okay, Mom." That broke the ice, and the other two boys followed, as Henry was the big brother. At last, we were a family.

It never occurred to me that it was hard for David and Bob, too, as I always thought they had their mother, and I was the security for them. I was wrong, as they had their own difficult adjustments to make.

I'm sure I made many mistakes, as hard as I tried.

Bob was everyone's scapegoat. He was the youngest and easy to pick on. He had the hardest time of all. He was angry, so much so that he would make holes in the wall and destroy his pillow, tossing feathers all over the room. I took him weekly to see a child psychologist in White Plains. We called him Goodie. I don't know how much it helped. Who knows! It might have started in the womb when I walked in on Miriam and Martin in bed together. But that was then, and this was now!

In my heart, I know that I accepted Henry, Jeff and Ken as my own. Although I know now that I did not make an effort to keep the memory of Joyce in their lives, I knew that she was with us and guiding me. In my mind I had a secret agreement with Joyce that she would watch over the children from heaven, and I would take care of them on earth. I thought of her often, as I felt inadequate to take her place, but I knew the children needed a mother. All I could offer them was love.

Florence, Joyce's mother, told my mother that if Joyce could come back and see how I was raising her boys, she would go back and rest peacefully. That meant so much to me. What a great lady she was.

I was not too good at discipline, but fortunately, except for some minor skirmishes between them, like when Henry would trip Ken on the steps, they were good kids.

I was certainly not an authority figure, and neither was Henry. He played tennis with the boys and ice skated with them, but he never 'fathered' them. He never asked them about their personal lives. He was affectionate but not warm. Henry only allowed *me* to see his inner self. He hid that part of himself from the whole world and was very stoic.

I, on the other hand, was an extrovert and bubbling over with warmth, but I was so insecure because of my early years that I was seeking approval my whole life.

Life was good!

The house was beautiful and so perfect for our large family. I used Thedlow, the same decorator as my father and Rose used, and they did a wonderful job.

The foyer led to a winding staircase with a high ceiling. I found a gorgeous chandelier that needed to be repainted. I rubbed it with black shoe polish to give it that old look. We had a large living room with a fireplace and a cozy den with a large window that overlooked the steep entrance with all the shrubs and tree tops. It had a window box that was planted with red geraniums. A large dining room adjoined a sunny glass-enclosed porch that we used as a breakfast room.

A few years later we added on an elongated bar room with windows overlooking the long driveway and gorgeous plantings. We also built an indoor/outdoor barbecue with a terrace to be able to eat outside. Off the driveway, we had a tennis court and free-form pool. In the winter, we would flood the tennis courts and ice skate. As a family, we had fun. The boys were great, and I loved my new family as though they had always been my own sons.

Halloween was a special time for us. I once decided to make a monster costume for Jeff. I got long johns for him and we all went to the chicken farm in Glenville to collect chicken feathers, which I proceeded to sew on his long underwear. That sure was not a good idea and did not go over too well.

Another time, Henry taught David and Jeff how to make bombs by scraping off match heads and putting them in small tins used for film, then attaching a string. Not exactly what a dad should be teaching his kids! The boys went out on Mischief Night.

It was a nice change from draping toilet paper around the neighborhood. They lit the fuse and tossed the bombs into mailboxes, then ran to watch the small explosions from a distance.

The problem was that the cops were out that night. They caught David and Jeff, put them against the side of the police car, and said, "Spread."

Needless to say, the boys were a little shaken and came home earlier than usual. The policeman was more forgiving, as, of course, they knew our name in the community. I remember asking the boys why they were home so early, and they answered, "Aw, Halloween is kid stuff." (So bored!)

Another Halloween, Jeff and David brought home a tombstone from an old country cemetery and put it at the front door. Not funny!

We also had German Shepherds. I did not want a dog, so Henry got together with the boys, and they bought me a puppy for my birthday. I was hooked after that.

Henry had been on one of his long trips. I picked him up very late at the airport in New York, and instead of going home, we went to the Plaza Hotel to have a little intimate time together. After breakfast we took a walk in Central Park, and I told him the good news. We were both hoping for a little girl, but when Craig was born, the doctor said, "I'm sorry, Marcy, it's another boy."

Craig cemented the family. The boys all adored him and treated him as their precious baby brother. I will always remember how happy Henry was when Craig was born.

During the last months of my pregnancy, I was with Henry in

Buenos Aires, visiting the company. They had built a factory for man-made fiber in Argentina. Henry's cousin Jerry Bibo was in charge of the office. Jerry was something of a playboy.

It was a wonderful time for us. We treated every trip as a honeymoon. I loved the Argentinean barbecue and corn cannelloni. I did not get on the plane to go home until my eighth month, and we met many wonderful Argentine friends.

But that was another mistake. I should have realized that the boys needed security. It had been a difficult transition for all of them. Henry, Jeff and Ken had been raised by the help. Henry did not spend much time with them, and their mother had died two years before.

All of a sudden, David and Bob had a new father and three new brothers, and I was thousands of miles away enjoying my new life and putting my own needs first.

I was hungry for love and did not want to be separated from Henry. I was selfish.

I had sent the boys to summer camp. That too was not wise.

The only redeeming feature was that mother and Lou were there most of the time, and they loved all the boys very much.

David and Jeff

Orchids by Marcy Von Kohorn

Chapter Eighteen

Chinese Brushwork

I did not have any talent for painting when I was young, and I do not remember being offered any art classes in school. Perhaps it was because there was no room in my troubled childhood for the peace in my soul that my new happiness now brought me....and yet, as a little girl, I would have a need for an outlet. So, I wrote about my life. My writings were often sad and created a world outside my world to which I would escape. It was as though the paper I wrote on was a substitution for a friend. I still write in a diary.

I would write pages of poetry and make a card for every occasion for my mother. One Mother's Day, I wrote inside a card, "Mother, you are, and always will be, the most precious gift God gave to me." My little poems were always accompanied with lilacs, Mother's favorite flower. I picked them from a neighbor's yard.

Another time, when I was in my teens, I drew a checkerboard on the outside of the card and inside wrote, "Your move, Valentine." I sold that one to Hallmark for $75.

I started taking watercolor lessons at the YWCA. I really did not get into it, as my teacher, Mr. Thompson, seemed to teach nothing but boats and houses.

One day after class, I was standing at the front door waiting for the heavy rain to stop when a lady joined me, and we chatted. She asked me if I would be interested in doing Chinese Brushwork. I had never heard of Chinese Brushwork but was intrigued. She took me to another floor to show me the class exhibit. Now I was more than intrigued. The gorgeous brushstrokes, the freedom, the rice paper, silk and gold leaf boards, and the beautifully painted flowers and landscapes. I knew this was what I wanted to do.

In 1960, I joined the class taught by Diana Kan, which became a big part of my life. I never missed a lesson and never missed a homework assignment. At first, I painted on the washing machine and dryer, as the surface had to be waist high and the artist had to stand while painting. We always started off by using freshly ground ink and doing Chinese calligraphy, sometimes just practicing strokes and sometimes characters. I could do pages and pages of calligraphy and never get tired. The strokes used in calligraphy were used in the paintings. Years later I turned one of the bedrooms into a studio.

Every Monday we met for classes at the YWCA, but then, as Miss Kan became more famous in the art world, we would drive into New York for lessons. Miss Kan would do a demonstration, and we copied it as homework. That was the learning technique that was practiced in Chinese painting for centuries by the old masters.

I found such joy in painting. Miss Kan arranged for us to have a show at the Pen and Brush Club in Greenwich Village, where we had our art classes. It was May and the flowering trees were pink and bursting with blossoms. I was so excited. I sold my first painting, flowers, of course.

Years later, when I had become a selling artist, Henry confessed that he had given someone the money to buy my painting. But I will never forget what a thrill it was. It was just like Henry to have done that to encourage me. I was even juried into the Pen and Brush Club.

When we were in New York for art lessons, we often had lunch in Chinatown and went snooping in the marvelous Oriental stores near 10th Street. I would take home a Peking duck, which everyone loved, and stuffed buns.

Miss Kan lived on 9th Street in Greenwich Village. She was married to Paul Schwartz, and they had one son by the name of Sing Si Schwartz. Sing had his mother's talent, but in photography, and became well known. He did portrait photos for many celebrities.

My painting was an important part of my life, Miss Kan became a dear friend to me, but even though we were close, we maintained the formal relationship of student and master. I always treated her with great respect.

When I painted, I seemed to be lifted to another planet. Even when I wasn't painting, images began to appear in my mind that would need to find expression.

She told us wonderful stories about Chinese culture and ancient painters. Miss Kan had studied with Chang Dai Chen from the time she was eight years old. He was considered to be one of the old masters.

She came to America when she was twenty years old and studied at the Art Students' League. She told us a wonderful story about having lunch with Sir Winston Churchill before he became Prime Minister of England. He and his wife Clementine were friends of her family.

It was during World War II. Just the three of them at the table, and Dame Clementine announced that she had picked strawberries from her Victory Garden for dessert. She also said that she had saved her sugar ration for the berries.

Miss Kan could not tell her that she was allergic to strawberries, so she ate them and just willed herself not to break out in a rash.

After the meal, Sir Winston said, "You know, Diana, there is no such thing as a free lunch." With that, he invited her upstairs to see his paintings. In ending the story, she said, "You know, we Chinese cannot lie."

Diana Kan was born in China, but when China was taken over by the Communists, her sister was murdered, their home was destroyed, and they fled to Taiwan, which had broken away from China. Chinese refugees lived on the island which they called the Republic of China. To this day, Mainland China and Taiwan remain bitter enemies.

Taiwan was a wonderful country to visit. When we were there, we stayed at the old, palatial Grand Hotel. When you walked into the white marble lobby and up the steps, you could smell the pungent odor of teak and incense. Their museum was so interesting, I could spend hours there.

Once, when I was in Taiwan with Henry on a business trip, I asked him if I could go to Hong Kong. He said of course, but I would have to go by myself. Before I boarded the plane to Hong Kong, Henry put lots of money in my hand; I said, "I'll never be able to spend so much." He replied, "Okay, just bring back what you don't spend."

I came back a week later with two dollars. Hong Kong was a shoppers' paradise.

Chapter Nineteen

Life in Greenwich

H enry had to travel a lot for his business and was often out of
the country for many weeks at a time. That was so hard for
both of us. We were newlyweds and longed to be together.
Often Henry would call me and ask me to meet him. It was a difficult
decision, as I knew the children needed me, and I wanted to be a good
mother to them. Of course, we did have Nanny. I did not know until
years later that the boys did not like her, but she and I worked very
well together as there were trips to school for pick up, doctors and
dentist appointments, driving to friends' houses and all the busyness
of a growing family.

Nanny was English, well organized, and I felt she was just strict
enough but not too much so. We also had Mickey, a Spanish woman
to work upstairs and to do laundry, and Celeste in the kitchen. I also
brought Juanita from Philadelphia. She had helped me when I lived
there.

Many times, Henry would phone me from the office in the
morning to inform me that we would be twelve for lunch. Most of his
clients were from India, Germany or Taiwan. I had to be very mindful
about dietary restrictions. Most of the Indians were vegetarians. His
clients were hugely wealthy and had many servants. They judged
Henry as worthy to do business with according to his style of living.

I learned to have whole meals ready to go, from the fish to the
dessert. My favorite soup, which they all raved about, was Campbell's
canned tomato soup mixed with pea soup, with a splash of Sherry,

served in a cup-sized bowl with toasted croutons. I always had a frozen bombe from the local bakery and their famous chocolate "Sarah Bernhardts" for dessert. We hired Julio to serve at the table in his starched white jacket, and he would drive when necessary.

When Henry would insist that I join him and my standard answer was, "I cannot leave the children," he would say, "Call your mother."

As I would go off to Paris, Bombay, Taiwan or some new and glamorous part of the world, mother always made it possible by being there with the children, whom she loved so much and whom they loved in return. It was always good to have grandma and grandpa there. Lou, who had been distant and cold to me, loved all the boys and was a wonderful grandfather to them.

In my life I had only one argument with my mother, who asked me to have David visit for the weekend. I agreed but then asked her when she would have Jeff? When she answered, "But Jeff is not my grandson," I told her that until she could accept all my children as her own, she would not be welcome in my home. That was hard, but mother did eventually love them all as her own.

Eventually, I legally adopted Henry, Jeff and Ken. Although Martin would never give permission to allow Henry to adopt David and Bob, when they were older, they requested the court to change that and were legally adopted by Henry. Martin agreed to fewer visitations when we agreed to let him stop his support payments ordered by the court.

We spent a lot of time with Ralph and Dee who became my best friend, and there was hardly a day we did not talk to each other. We were a happy foursome—Ralph and Dee and Henry and me.

Ralph and Dee had two children, Stephen and Karen. Ralph had made it clear that he did not like children, that he did not want any of his own and was never much of a father.

Henry's father Oscar was president of the Von Kohorn International Corp and had been a very successful industrialist. Known as The Baron, Vati was credited with inventing the rayon process. Their home in Chemnitz, Germany was more like a castle, with many acres of beautiful grounds, a caretaker's cottage, a swimming pool and tennis court. Everything was confiscated by the Nazis.

Business interests took them to Japan for two years and then to America.

Oscar re-established the family in New York in the business of man-made fiber. The company had an excellent international reputation, so much so that they became a rival to DuPont.

Vati was a gentle man and a gentleman. He was brilliant, kind and devoted to his wife and two sons. He welcomed me into the family. I always loved him.

As the years passed, Henry felt that his father should retire, and that Henry should assume the title and the responsibilities of president. This caused a breach in their relationship, and Vati was put out to pasture.

Henry did a great job as president but almost single handedly. Although he had a great staff, including experts, an in-house lawyer, not to mention secretaries and office staff, Henry was the only one to negotiate contracts and to keep the company organized. He became friends with all his clients. Most of them were house guests and entertained by us. Ralph became vice-president.

The company had offices in Bombay, Tokyo and Buenos Aires. They built their own building in White Plains, New York, known as the Von Kohorn building. The payroll was enormous, but then so was the profit when the synthetic fiber rolled off the (patented) machinery at each plant in thirty different countries.

Many times, Ralph and Dee and Henry and I would be sitting around the bar having drinks and hors d'oeuvres and the two brothers would be excited about still another expert they hired away from DuPont. When I felt this knot in my stomach, perhaps a premonition and warned them not to tweak the toe of a giant, my warnings were dismissed. What did I know!

Chapter Twenty

Henry's Inventions

Henry was a member of the United States Lawn Tennis Association and entered tournaments wherever and whenever he could. He went nowhere in the world without his racquet. In 1948, Henry played doubles in an indoors tournament in New York City. His partner was Dr. Reginald Weir, the first African American accepted by the ELTA.

In 1972, he had a national senior ranking in singles of 26 and was ranked #1 in New England.

In Australia, Henry played with Harry Hopman, the famous Davis Cup coach of the Australian Team. He and Harry became good friends. When Harry moved to the US, he was our house guest (more like family) for almost a year.

Henry was also an inventor. He invented a synthetic sponge for which he created a company called Nylonge. He also invented the Rescue Pad which ended up on the shelf of every grocery store in the country. We received royalties for the Rescue Pad for twenty years.

He invented a table he called "the Barbecenter." It was a table with a grill in the middle and a hot plate surrounding the grill, with an eating surface surrounding the entire table. There was a gas tank underneath to heat the table and a bench for guests to sit on. I would set out a table of raw meat, parboiled potatoes, eggs, onions and some vegetables. Our guests would select what they wanted and with long-handled forks and spatulas, they cooked the food on the grill and hot plate. It was great fun and a wonderful way to entertain, but the

Barbecenter never went commercial.

Henry also had a patent on a method of lighting that was subtle and beautiful. It was called Moodlite.

Craig believed so much in the patents that he and Kathy moved to Vero Beach shortly after they were married so that he could help his father and become part of the company. He studied all the patents and became knowledgeable about the claims. He worked hard on Moodlite, and the homes and companies which had the installations were thrilled with the results.

Moodlite could be used outdoors to illuminate landscapes with a subtle non-glare light to take the place of the bright bullet bulbs being used on most properties. It could also be used to illuminate indoor plants, giving a room a romantic and soft lighting effect.

The outdoor landscape lighting was most popular. Craig created some beautiful installations, but he could not do it all. He sold the business in 1990.

Craig worked closely with Henry. He was very familiar with the patents and became an important part of the business and a manager.

I think of Kathy as "superwoman." She is a wonderful mother, worked for Merrill Lynch, and always had good food on the table for her little family. She started the job one week before she found out she was pregnant with Kyle.

Despite his genius, Henry did not like to use the computer. He spoke French, German, Spanish and some Japanese and was fascinated with astronomy and the studies of the galaxies and outer space.

He was sent to the University of Michigan by the army during the war and learned over four thousand kanji. He was in intelligence and was very proud of the maps he drew for General Patton.

Chapter Twenty-one

Paris

The first time Henry took me to Paris, we stayed at the George Cinq Hotel. Wouldn't you know it was raining? I caught a bad cold, felt miserable and had to stay in bed.

Henry asked me who my favorite couturier was. I had seen some designs in Vogue by Desas, so that was my answer. Desas used lovely folds and drapes. Henry then surprised me. As I sat up in the beautiful four poster bed, he arranged for seven models from Desas to parade before me as they changed into elegant cocktail dresses in the bathroom.

I was to pick any dress to be made to order for me. Henry liked a bright red dress with a small train, which was very glamorous, but I felt a black dress was more practical. And so, I had made a gorgeous black silk organza dress with three quarter sleeves that looked like black roses. The back was cut down to the waist. I loved it and could never believe that Henry could do something so thoughtful. He could think of so many ways to make me happy.

That was the first of many trips to Paris, which became one of our meeting places when Henry was "sitting" out a contract somewhere.

I was grateful to Mrs. Neighbors, Henry's personal secretary who made all my travel arrangements. I would board the plane, which in those days was not a jet, and after dinner go to the bathroom, change into my nightie, climb up into my sleeping berth with instructions to the stewardess to wake me an hour before landing.

On one trip to Paris, the Paris airport was fogged in so we could not land. It was a Pan American flight, and they had to land us in Brussels. We were then put on a train to Paris, but the airline had lost my luggage. As I boarded the train, I passed a compartment with four men who, on seeing me, got my attention and beckoned me to join them. They explained that I should not go any further, as the Russians were in the next compartment, so I settled in for the ride to Paris with them.

After their initial greeting, they "talked business," and it seemed to me (with my active imagination) that they were some big shots from the government. They spoke very freely about plans in front of me, and I was sure that the gentleman with the English accent and the leather patches on his tweed jacket was an English spy!

When they broke to go to dinner in the dining car, there was an empty seat at our table. The maître d' showed one of the Russians to our table to join us, and he uttered a very definite "Nyet." (*No* in Russian).

When we arrived in Paris, this group of men, who had been very protective of me, each gave me their business cards and invited me to call them if I encountered any problem. When I looked at the cards later, I found that one was a Brigadier General and one was the head of the World Bank.

I took a taxi to the hotel, but of course it was raining, and when I arrived, I certainly looked worn and forlorn, my hair bedraggled, no luggage and wet through and through. Henry was not there yet. He and the lost luggage arrived the next day. He did not quite believe my story until I produced the calling cards.

The summer of 1960 we took the glamorous Queen Elizabeth from New York to Cherbourg, France, where we rented a car and drove from one *Guide-Michelin* four-star restaurant to the next, passing charming French towns and villages through the colorful countryside. We drove to the Eden Roc Hotel in Du Cap D' Antibes on the French Riviera and stayed until it was time to go to Rolle, the school in which we had enrolled Henry Jr. for a summer course to learn French. There was a business trip to Paris. Many of the staff were with us on this trip, so we stayed at the Westminster Hotel. I asked Henry to take me to Montmartre, the art district of Paris. I did want to buy another painting but could not find an artist whose work

I liked. I bought a black and white oil by Brusset. It was a painting of the fountain in front of the Louvre.

At Montmartre, I found an artist whose work I liked, but there was no painting that I liked enough to buy.

When we got back to the hotel, I told Henry that I would look him up in the telephone directory. Henry thought that was very funny. He said, "Oh yes, you don't speak French and you are just going to call him on the phone." I said, "Yes, that's exactly what I am going to do." And that is what I did. Luigi Corbelinni answered the phone, and I explained to him that I was an American and that I would like to come to see his work. He invited us, in his wonderful French accent, to come to a cocktail party he was having that evening. I had a hard time convincing Henry to go, but we did go to the party and took Ira with us. Ira was an attorney, young and good looking. When we arrived at the door, Luigi explained that he was very poor because his wife left him and took everything he owned, including all his paintings.

Luigi was wearing jeans and a white shirt with a pair of yellow socks pinned together and made into an ascot. Alongside him was a tall beautiful Oriental woman, obviously his girlfriend. It was fun to meet so many interesting, artistic and bohemian people.

As each of the guests left, the three of us were the only ones still there. It was not easy to keep Henry and Ira there so long. Luigi invited us to dinner. Henry was not happy but went along to please me. Luigi took us to a restaurant in a section of Paris that was very colorful. To me, it looked like a Lautrec painting, with sawdust on the floor and waitresses with heavy rouged cheeks. The menus had two items to choose from, so we all had jackass steak at a dollar-fifty and lots and lots of Vodka.

Luigi's girlfriend was sitting next to Ira, and it was obvious that she was taken by this young American. Luigi was not happy about this, but when she took the pickle off her plate and put it on Ira's plate, he really became upset. The party broke up and turned into a Russian tragedy as Corbellini angrily shouted, "With my last sous I invite you to dinner and you try to steal my girlfriend."

The next day I asked Henry to send him a bottle of Scotch and to ask him to paint my portrait. We offered him five hundred dollars.

There was another cocktail party as I sat on the dais with Luigi painting my portrait. I arrived in a black shirt which he asked me to remove. He gave me a bulky yellow sweater and draped a green scarf from the piano over me. It took him four hours to paint my portrait.

I will always love that painting.

Marcy At the Eden Roc Hotel

Chapter Twenty-two

Russia

In 1925 VKIC had put up a synthetic fiber plant in the Soviet Union. The plant was located in a small town outside of Moscow. The company was asked to modernize the plant, as the machinery by then was quite old.

We stayed at the Moscow Hotel, which faced Red Square, and every day there was a long line of people waiting to see Lenin encased in a glass coffin.

When I went on a tour, the guide took me to their famous Guam Department Store. We passed a magnificent cathedral, and I asked the guide if anyone worshiped there. She answered, "Only the old and the ignorant."

I decided to ride on the bus to see the sights on my own. An older man also riding the bus approached me and handed me a small piece of paper on which was written, "Please give this to your President Eisenhower. The Russian people want peace." I kept that small piece of paper for many years. I guess, in the scheme of things, it is always "the people" who pay the price for the political heads of state and their greed.

I took my paints on this trip and went to the Kremlin hoping to set up and paint. Each time I came to a guard with a red arm band, I was instructed to open my case. The guard would make me stop until he squeezed each paint tube to be sure it was paint. Needless to say, I could not do any painting.

No matter where we went, of course, Henry traveled with his

tennis racquet and looked for a game. He lost no time in calling the British Embassy, and he made friends with Chris McAlpine, attached to the embassy. Every morning Chris would send a car and driver to pick up Henry. We then noticed that our room was bugged, and we were being followed.

We spent many pleasant evenings in the embassy with Chris and Helen. They showed me the wire, which was hidden under the inlay on the dining room floor. I asked why they did not pull it out. She explained that this way they knew where it was.

We were invited to a luncheon at the plant. The entourage was quite impressive with a long line of limos. We were entertained quite royally. There were many Russian officials, the VKIC staff, a few experts from our English counterpart and our in-house lawyer.

We were given a magnificent luncheon, and the Vodka flowed quite freely. Each time the whisky glass was filled there was a toast that sounded like "Za Vashee Zda Ro Vye." Most of the members of our group were sophisticated enough not to empty their glasses, but poor John Peek, a charming young English engineer drank it down each time and ended up with alcohol poisoning, which was pretty serious. The Russians took him to the infirmary there and forced tea down his throat from an old soiled bag that looked like it was from World War I. They no doubt saved his life!

Chapter Twenty-three

Travel

VKIC had also built a plant in a small town called Kafr el Dawwar near Cairo, Egypt. The company engaged in designing, installing and the operation of rayon, staple fiber and nylon plants.

When Henry and I visited the plant there, it was like something from a different world. We spent the night in a beautiful guesthouse. It was in the desert, isolated and very romantic. When the sun went down, the stars seemed to hang so low in the sky that I could reach out and touch them. There was the sound of a coyote baying in the moonlight.

The manservants served us a delicious dinner and attended to our every need. They seemed to anticipate what we would like before we even thought of it, each one in the same robe and fez hat with a tassel hanging down the side and walking so silently that I could not hear a step.

Henry had a way of enticing me to join him wherever he went.

When he had to be in Tokyo for a few weeks, he sent me a picture of an exquisite string of Mikimoto pearls displayed on a black velvet background. He told me that they were waiting for me in customs, but if I did not come, they would be returned to the shop.

We stayed at the beautiful Imperial Hotel. There was an old section to the hotel with small doors and Japanese style furniture and beds. There was also a luxurious modern section for Westerners.

We went to sushi bars and also to a tea house with Geisha girls.

We visited the imposing Japanese temples and went to a tea ceremony. I was fascinated to see the beautifully arranged flower arrangements for which the Japanese are so famous. I love to arrange flowers and seem to do it so easily. We also went to Kabuki, a classical Japanese play where all the parts were played by men.

Henry was able to understand Japanese and to speak to the waiter, the taxi driver and everyone in Japanese.

The company also built and supplied machinery to a plant in Taiwan and many times we went there from Tokyo. We always had the same corner suite at the Grand Hotel and, of course, Henry would immediately order his Peking duck.

Chapter Twenty-four

Visitors from India

Henry often invited visitors to stay with us. Everyone's favorite was Nannubhai. I will never forget his face the first time he saw snow. Nannubhai was the official jeweler of all the maharaja and maharini in India. He also worked with the famous Harry Winston jeweler on Fifth Ave.

Once when he was our guest, he invited us to go to New York to meet the Maharaja and Maharini of Gwalior at the Waldorf Towers.

We met in the suite in which they were staying and quickly became friends. They had their daughter, Padma, with them. Padma was about seventeen and beautiful. She and her mother had been shopping downstairs at the Waldorf, where they bought a lovely red chiffon cocktail dress for Padma. We had reservations at "21" for dinner and her mother tried to persuade her to wear her new dress, with no success. She then suggested, "If Marcy wears sari, will you wear the red dress?"

Padma agreed. Fortunately, I wore a black satin suit with a matching shell top. I was given a gorgeous black sari with a wide red hem and hand-sewn red and gold-shaped diamonds embroidered on the luscious silk. It was wrapped around me and around my head. The dot, which was worn by Indian ladies, was placed on my forehead. The black shell top was perfect with it. The restaurant was so internationally famous, I was quite comfortable in my lovely sari.

Padma was engaged to a maharaja whom she had only met once and did not like. I tried to convince her parents to allow her to stay with us in Greenwich for a few months to have a taste of freedom and the warmth our little family could give her, but to no avail. When she returned to India, she and I corresponded faithfully. She wrote to me on her wedding day, as she sat up "in the tower" watching the parade of elephants, giraffes and camels with men marching and dressed in elaborate costumes.

Padma then had two sons. Even though we continued to write to each other, I never knew how unhappy she was, until I learned that she committed suicide.

Henry and I visited with Nannubhai in Bombay, which is now Mumbai. They had a holy man who lived with them. His head was shaved, and he sat bare chested on the floor with his legs crossed, meditating.

The punji advised Nannubhai about business matters and what his lucky days and numbers were.

The Indian people do not kill any living thing. They think it may be one of their ancestors. When we were sitting in their living room a mouse was scooting across the floor. I tucked my feet up under me, and Henry gave me a look that meant, "Keep quiet." I did. The mouse did not seem to bother anyone else.

When Nannubhai first became interested in having a factory built, he was going to deal with an Italian firm.

The pundit told him there was no need to go to Italy as he would be partnered with an American firm. Nannubhai still took a flight to Italy and sat next to a member of the VKIC staff on the plane. They exchanged information. The deal with Italy fell through, and VKIC built the synthetic fiber plant for him.

When they signed the contract in White Plains, it had to be signed at a designated time and with his lucky flower, marigolds, which were impossible to buy. I climbed a fence to pick them and produced the flowers at the exact minute dictated by the holy man.

Chapter Twenty-five

Vienna

Of any place we ever visited, Vienna was my favorite. Vienna was part of Henry's life, a city of love and a city of music. It was the city where Johann Strauss Jr. played his melodic waltzes for Emperor Franz Joseph. It was a city that echoed the sounds of music everywhere.

Henry's mother was an operetta star there, and Henry was raised with music. He sat on Richard Strauss's lap as a little boy. Many of the great singers and composers visited their home.

The night we arrived, we took our bags to the hotel and ran to the Volks-opera. Even though it was all in German, I was able to understand most of the words. The songs, the whole performance, were like magic.

Henry told me what part his mother had played. He sat there enthralled. I could see Vienna in Henry and Henry in Vienna. It helped me to understand his love of music, his gentleness, his wonderful sense of humor and his "bon appetite."

We strolled down the wide street closed to traffic and lined with shops and restaurants, where you could buy all kinds of sausages, bratwursts and mugs of cool exhilarating beer.

We arranged to get tickets to hear the famous choirboys. Their voices were amazing. Unfortunately, our seats were behind a huge pillar and I could not see the singers or the chapel.

I was determined to see the magnificent chapel and went there the next day but found it was closed to the public as there was a wedding that day. I went in as a wedding guest. The chapel was indeed impressive, but so was the wedding, which took place on the stage. The couple each sat in a chair facing the priest who conducted the wedding ceremony. A man sitting next to me kept speaking to me in German, and although I understood some, but certainly not enough to carry on a conversation, I just kept saying, "ach ya." As we all exited after the ceremony, I went through the reception line and shook hands with the bride and groom.

Returning to the hotel, I came across a line waiting to get into a building. I decided to see what that was all about. It was an entrance to see the apartments of the princess. The apartment was very beautiful, but what impressed me the most was a large and extremely well-equipped gym.

The hotel was small and very quaint. It was called the Hotel Astoria and had lovely lace curtains at the windows. I loved the feel of this place. The rooms were light and airy. I preferred it to the famous tourist Hotel Imperial.

When we checked in, the owners recognized the name and told us that Henry's parents had stayed there often.

Henry told me about the time he and his brother Ralph were together and traveling through the Black Forest. They found an old dilapidated building they remembered to have been the glamorous theater where their mother had performed. It was evening and just turning dark. They knocked on the door, wondering if anyone would be there. An old hunchbacked man answered the door. They explained that they were hoping to find some posters of their mother's appearance and that she had been a famous operetta singer in 1905. The keeper took them up to the attic, which was covered with cobwebs, and, after looking through many posters, they did find the ones of Mutti, which we treasure. They are hanging on my wall.

On a business trip to Munich, Germany, I decided to go to Salzburg and boarded the train. Henry, back at a meeting, wondered to himself whether I remembered to take my passport and then thought, "Well, let the Austrians take care of themselves." Of course, I had not taken my passport, and when the conductor came around and said, "Passports, bitte." I replied, "I did not bring my passport, but I am an American." "No matter," he answered in broken English.

"When we arrive in Salzburg you must go back."

I was not one to be discouraged. I stood in the aisle outside the compartment where I noticed the conductor looking out the window. I said, "Do you speak English?" He answered, "Ya, ein little." I asked, "Are you married?" "Ya," he answered.

"Do you have children?" I asked, as I motioned with my hands. "Ya," he answered." "Do you have pictures?" I asked. The conductor proudly took photos from his pocket to show me two little girls. "Schön," I exclaimed. He then showed me a picture of his wife. By the time we reached Salzburg, we had become friends. "Do you have any form of identification?" he asked.

"I have an Exon credit card with my picture on it," I replied as I pulled out my card, ever hopeful. "Okay," he said, "but only to allow you a day pass. You must leave at the end of the day, and I will be here to be sure you do."

I thanked him profusely and proceeded to explore Salzburg, the home of Mozart.

Peace by Marcy Von Kohorn

Chapter Twenty-six

Washington DC

Henry was interested in building another plant for his company in the Soviet Union, and there was an important Russian delegation meeting in Washington.

With all the foreign trips I took, I had never been anywhere in my own country and was anxious to see Washington. Henry went to Washington and called me to meet him there to be a hostess at a dinner party he was giving. He told me to meet him at the Mayflower Hotel.

Julio drove me to the airport, and Nanny and Craig went along for the ride. On the way to the airport, we got a flat tire. I took my suitcase and put up my thumb for someone to pick me up and get me to the airport on time. A nice gentleman picked me up and got me to the airport with seconds to spare.

Once at the hotel in Washington, I went to the front desk to inquire about Henry's room. The desk clerk told me there was no one registered by that name. I did not know what to do. I sat in the lobby, thinking maybe he would come into the hotel. It was close to seven o'clock and our guests were due at seven. I went to the house phone and asked the operator to connect me to Henry's room. He answered the phone and of course was very upset, as I was so late. The dinner party went off fine, like a play, but who knows what goes on backstage.

Henry had meetings, so I signed up to go on a tour to the White House. It was an interesting tour and we ended up at the Senate Reception room. I remember that I was wearing a black chesterfield

109

coat with a white scarf and gloves.

We were told that President Nixon and the ambassador from the Soviet Union were together in the room. We waited outside in hopes of seeing the President.

Shortly after, the president and Mr. Zuruban came out together, smiling and appearing to be best friends. The President stopped in front of me and said, "Hello, young lady. Are you a student?" I answered, "No, Mr. President, I am the mother of six children."

He asked me where I was from. When I told him I was from Connecticut, he said, "Well, Connecticut must be a very prolific state."

Henry was trying to get an appointment with a man by the name of Mikoyan, who was important in the Soviet Union, but he was unable to contact him. On the train returning to Connecticut we saw him sitting in the parlor car next to the one we were in. I went to the next car, sat down beside him and engaged him in conversation. After a while, Henry followed. I introduced them and gave my seat to Henry.

Chapter Twenty-seven

Family Life

To explain this interruption in time and in my narrative, I would like to describe the lives of our children here. Families grow up and become adults. They try different careers, form new bonds and then birth their own children. Our sons were probably the most important part of our lives together and continue to be throughout my lifetime.

We were caught up in the highly unpopular Vietnam War. Our son Henry, who had just graduated from Princeton, enlisted in the army. I can still feel the terrible grip around my heart when we drove him to the induction center; however, God was with him when he went through training at Fort Dix. He was at the top of his class and had a choice of an assignment. He ended up in Italy, where he met Meredith Forinash, whom he married in 1970. I gave a huge party for them to celebrate their engagement. I loved having Meredith as a daughter-in-law

Our son Henry weds Meredith

and still do to this day. They were married in York, Pennsylvania.

Young Henry worked first for an insurance company in investments and then for Goldman Sachs. After many years, he left Goldman and opened his own successful real estate company

Henry and Meredith have two daughters. They lived for many years in Westport Connecticut on a gorgeous estate. Henry remained active as a Princeton alumnus in volunteer work for the University and then moved to Princeton with Meredith, where he is still being challenged by academia.

Ken's first marriage was to Judy Mullins, who was the daughter of our good friends Jack and Jane Mullins. The marriage did not work out, and he and Judy got a divorce.

Ken graduated from Yale and is an investment counselor. It comes easy to him, and he gradually acquired clients.

Ken continued with his investment firm and remained successful. He met Sue Bonnar on a train trip from New York. She seemed charming and was very pretty, but it happened too fast. I begged Ken to give it more time, but I remember that he told me that "Sue is perfect." He built a large and beautiful home in Westport overlooking a lake. He and Sue had three sons and a daughter.

After many years Ken informed the family that he and Sue would be getting a divorce. Ken was a bachelor for some time but finally met the right woman and is happily married to Dana McBride.

David was married to Joanne Loulan, who was a strong feminist. They opened a store in Colorado called Folk's Art. After several years David and Joanne were divorced.

David lived in Menlo Park and remained a bachelor for years. He met Lisa O'Brien, and they had a lovely wedding in a charming spot next to a babbling brook on a warm summer day in August. They have a daughter by the name of Zoe.

David is very creative. He first went to Boston University and then got a degree in fine arts from the University of San Francisco.

He moved to Palo Alto, California, and ended up with one of the largest architectural signage and graphic shops in the Bay Area of San Francisco. While producing signs that were prominent in outstanding places such as Stanford University and well-established business locations, David took courses in psychology and got a degree from the

Institute of Transpersonal Psychology. He never stopped his studies. He got his master's in counseling and became a psychotherapist.

David and Lisa and Zoe moved to Ashville, North Carolina, where David now has a private practice in which he treats individuals, couples and families. Lisa continues her career in nursing.

Jeff married Nancy Lakeman, and they lived in San Diego. They had two sons. Nancy went to her college reunion and met the man who was her first love. She left Jeff, and her first love left his wife so that they could be married.

Nancy gave up custody of Dan and Jon. Jeff raised the boys and was the best "Dr. Mom" one could imagine.

Jeff went to Northwestern University and received a degree in psychology. He moved back to Connecticut and met Elizabeth Bergen, who was perfect for Jeff and for the boys, who love her.

Jeff works at Fairfield Country Day School and is valued in his specialty as a child psychologist. Jeff plays table tennis and enters tournaments whenever he can. He is even teaching the boys at the school table tennis.

Bob graduated from Georgetown in Washington D.C. with a business degree and received an MBA from the University of Bridgeport. He became a manager and director of a major TV system, starting at Westinghouse, and is still working in the industry.

He came home one night shortly after graduating from college and was love struck, as he had met "the most beautiful girl in the world" the night before. He married Dana Howard as soon as he graduated and is still married to her. They have two daughters, Olivia and Melody.

Craig went to Proctor Academy in New Hampshire and Pace University, where he graduated with a business degree. He worked at the Marriott Hotel in Stamford, Connecticut, where he met Kathleen Johns. They were married in Endicott, N.Y. He and Kathy moved to Vero Beach, Florida, so Craig could help Henry with his patents. They have a son and a daughter.

This little family has been near and dear to me for over 30 years. Kathy is like a daughter to me. Craig is now a realtor with Alex MacWilliam.

Chapter Twenty-eight

The End of VKIC

One evening when Henry and I were sitting at the dinner table with the boys, the phone rang. I got up to answer the phone, which was in the den. It was a reporter from the New York Times. He asked me if I had any comment about the lawsuit against Von Kohorn International Corporation by DuPont for the use of trade secrets. I remember going back to the dinner table and almost choking on the food, but I did not say a word about the call until Henry and I were alone. I guess that was the end of my fairy tale.

The litigation went on for five years and was handled by a prominent firm from New York. Henry had often sent out memos to his staff to remind them that, "We do not want your trade secrets."

We lost the case, as trade secrets were discovered in the Argentine office of Gerry Bibo. There was no defense. I often thought about the way Henry and Ralph hired experts from DuPont! In December 1966, the New York Times printed an article that, after a five-year-old damage suit against Von Kohorn International Corporation, E.I. DuPont announced that they had accepted a settlement of $6.8 million. VKIC had been charged with unfair competition and misappropriation of trade secrets.

Those were difficult years, and although Henry never discussed business with me, I knew he was struggling, and I knew he felt personally responsible for what had happened. Henry had such integrity that I knew this was a terrible blow to his self-esteem.

Gradually things went downhill, and the company went out of business. The debts were enormous, and Henry was left to face this catastrophe alone.

Ralph and Dee had marriage problems before this happened. Dee left him, took the children and went back to Australia. Ralph was devastated and tried to commit suicide. He had some contacts in New Zealand and went there to start a new life.

There he met Jill who was then only 21 years old and had her own school of deportment called the Academy of Excellence. They seemed to be made for each other, and she was thrilled to be a baroness. They used the title wherever they went. Ralph bought a beautiful yacht and sailed the Marlborough Sound. He became a commodore and wrote a book on boating.

Ralph of course had no family expenses. He invested his money and did well. He took Jill to all the embassy parties, and they loved the prestige.

Life was not the same for us. There were no more brand-new automobiles on the driveway with big red bows for Christmas. There were no more pleasure trips abroad for us. Henry sold his interest in Nylonge for three hundred and fifty dollars to his manager.

We sold our home on Pecksland Road, with its swimming pool and tennis court, for less than it was worth and moved into a more modest home on Perkins Road. It was still a lovely house, and we were happy there, even though I heard there was a lot of gossip.

We had no more sources of income, except what Henry was able to save. We certainly did not suffer. We were still collecting royalties on Henry's invention of the Rescue Pad. We still belonged to the Burning Tree Country Club. We still gave elegant parties, and Craig, Jeff, David and Bob still went to Greenwich Country Day School.

We no longer had an upstairs maid and downstairs maid or cook. I was it. We had our wonderful Rose who came to clean once a week.

The worst part of those years for me was to watch Henry trying to make a living. He got a job with Bangor Punta in Greenwich as an international adviser. He then got a job at Healthchem, which made insecticides. Henry was a chemical engineer and contributed a very important invention to them but got nothing for if as it was on company time. He was still on the Board at Union Trust Bank, and he was also on the board of the World Trade Center. According to the settlement with DuPont, he wasn't permitted to work in the synthetic fiber field.

Chapter Twenty-nine

New Zealand

Ralph and Jill came often to see us in Connecticut and to see Mutti, who by then was getting old. Jill was everyone's favorite, and the family looked forward to their visits. They always came to our Christmas parties and to family events like graduations and weddings. I became very fond of Jill.

We were like sisters. Henry and I went to visit them in New Zealand, and they gave a wonderful welcome party in our honor. It was then that we met Dick and Rhoda Potton, who became our dear friends.

We went boating on the Marlborough Sound on Ralph's boat, with Dick and Rhoda following in theirs. Jill cooked incredible meals onboard. Henry did not like being on a boat, but I loved it. I even set up my paints and did a lovely small painting while we were moored.

Welcome Party in New Zealand

On Ralph's boat one

117

evening we decided to go to a restaurant to give our gourmet chef (Jill) a night off. We girls put on our finest and, with high heels and looking very glamorous, took the dingy to shore and dined at a charming restaurant situated among the holiday cottages. When it was time to go back to the boat, Henry announced that he had booked a cottage and refused to spend another uncomfortable night on Ralph's boat.

In my small purse, I had nothing but a comb and lipstick! We agreed to meet down at the dock in the morning. The dock was quite a distance from the cottage and when we awoke the next morning, it was raining heavily. The paths had turned to mud, and we had no choice but to run for it.

We stopped off briefly at the restaurant, and I was able to get some bread wrappers from the kitchen, which I put on my head and feet. I heard one comment, "Look at those crazy Americans." Our clothes were plastered to us, and we were wringing wet. We never spent another night on Ralph's boat!

I noticed on that trip that Rhoda had some health issues. One night when we were out, she felt dizzy. We went to the ladies' room where there was a chaise lounge, and she rested awhile. Some months later, Rhoda died of cancer. It was tragic, and we all mourned her passing. She was a lovely, elegant, beautiful and caring wife and mother. Dick was devastated.

Henry and Marcy in New Zealand

Dick suffered with post-polio. He carried himself listing to one side and could not turn his head. He had no use of his arm and had to move it using his one good arm. Dick was one of the brightest, most talented men I have ever met. He made his fortune transporting the refrigerated fish to Kobe, Japan, where they cherish their raw fish.

It was around the Christmas holidays, and I knew how lonesome he was, so we asked him to come spend time with us. By then, we had moved to Florida, and Dick and I walked the beach and spent some time at Disney. He always remained one of our closest friends.

Henry, Marcy and Dick Potton at Disney World

Chapter Thirty

Egypt

In 1979, Henry was asked by Chase Manhattan Bank to teach a course in International Business at the graduate level to students in Cairo, Egypt. It was the year that President Anwar Sadat met in Cairo with President Carter and Mr. Begin, the prime minister of Israel, to sign a peace treaty.

What a wonderful dream come true for the whole world, and how exciting to be there at that time.

Henry loved teaching this class, and the students loved him. I spent time with him in Egypt but would go back and forth, not wanting to be away from the boys too long, though they were grown by then. I remember seeing such poverty that I could not believe people could live that way. Their houses were made of cow dung, and I saw children eating grass. They were laughing and playing though on the banks of the Nile.

I visited The City of the Dead, where people buried their families. They owned a house there and visited relatives who had passed on as though they were still alive.

I visited the famous bazaar (Khan el-Khalili) where you could buy anything you wanted but were expected to haggle. Henry used to tell a story about when he was negotiating a contract in Egypt. Mr. Mohamed said, "But Mr. Von Kohorn, you have to bring the price down." Henry then said, "But Mr. Mohamed, I have not given you a price yet."

The streets were teeming with all kinds of people—beggars,

people selling things, urchins tugging at you for a coin, men urinating in the gutter. There were donkey carts next to autos, next to buses with people hanging out of the windows and holding on to the sides of the bus.

I went to the magnificent Cairo Museum where mummies were encased in gold. I saw gloves, clothing and jewelry that were thousands of years old.

Henry did not like to go sightseeing and had been there many times, so I went everywhere myself. I took a plane to Karnack, where columns of antiquity stood defying time. The Sphinx lined the ancient road where Cleopatra had walked.

I met a Japanese man and a Polish woman. We became friends and met for dinner every night. I saw the tombs and went underground in the pyramids where pharaohs buried their wives, servants and treasures with them and prepared their boat to sail down the Nile to eternity when they died. There were paintings on the walls using pigment ground from semi-precious stones. The same pigment is used in Chinese paint today.

I went to the "Sound of Light," the light show put on at the pyramids at night, and I rode a camel on the desert sands. Fatma and Hassan Nagy were dear friends, and we practically lived in their flat even though we were staying in the El Salaam Hotel. They treated us like family. Many times, I spent time painting there, and Fatma loved my work.

She said to me, "We know the most famous artist in Egypt. His name is Salah Tahar. If you bring your paintings each time you come here, I will ask him to look at them, and maybe he will sponsor you in a show."

And so it happened. One day I lined up 20 of my paintings against the wall in their apartment, and we waited for Salah to appear. He was a handsome man with shocking white hair like a lion's mane and a thick white mustache.

As he walked around the room looking at my paintings, it seemed like an eternity. Finally, he said, "I like your work. I would like to sponsor you in a show with my son, Ayman." I was ecstatic. And so it all started!

The opening was set for the second of April, our wedding

anniversary. As I sat in the lobby of the luxurious El Salam Hotel, watching the signing of the peace treaty in Washington on TV, I was thrilled, although the news was all in Arabic. I understood though that Mr. Begin and President Carter accepted an invitation from Mr. Sadat to visit Egypt.

We delivered two hundred invitations to the opening of the art show by hand as mail was unreliable. We visited with many dignitaries as we handed out the invitations. Ayman would introduce me as his American friend who did Chinese brush work. Everyone accepted with the understanding that they could not come if Mr. Begin was to arrive that day.

As luck would have it, the date of his visit turned out to be the very day of our opening. Begin's arrival was kept very quiet until the last minute. The first we knew of it was when we were notified that our hotel would be vacated for him and for his contingent from April 1 to April 3. Hotel rooms were almost impossible to come by in Cairo on short notice, so we found a second-rate hotel, which was pretty bad, but we were lucky to have found anything at all.

We hung the show on Sunday, April 1; and Monday, April 2 turned out to be 100 degrees, completely unseasonable for that time of year. Everyone was undone by the heat. On the day of our opening, the elevator broke down, the door key did not work in the lock, and there was no electricity and no water in the hotel.

It amazes me that we got to the show in one piece. The Cairo traffic, which is usually bad, was impossible, snarled by the usual donkey carts, overcrowded buses and bumper to bumper cars, in addition to the excitement of Mr. Begin being in Cairo. No one seemed to know where. Most of the Egyptians I spoke to at different social levels were thrilled at having peace with Israel.

At the opening, a white ribbon had been placed across the entrance and was cut by Dr. Abdel Kadar Matem, head of the National Specialized Cultural Council. We had over one hundred guests, despite the absence of government officials. The press and the public received us enthusiastically. I was interviewed on the Voice of America, but it was broadcast in Arabic. We were on TV, and several newspapers and magazines had articles about us.

Briefly, I became something of a celebrity and met so many

fascinating people in the art world. Salah Tahar did turn out to be the most famous artist in Egypt, as he was chosen to paint the poster for the Peace Treaty.

Shortly after our return to the States, we sold our home on Perkins Road for $600,000. (It is now worth $4 million). We rented a house in Stamford. Henry hated the house. He said it was dark and ugly. And so it was, but it helped that we were able to keep our furniture in it. I kept all the boxes of china, linens, books, etc. in the attic. Craig's friends helped us with the move.

I continued painting and continued my trips to New York with my art friends. Life went on. It was around Christmas time, and I had the family over for our Christmas dinner, but I was nursing a bad case of the shingles. It was in my eyelid and down the back of my head and was very painful.

Shortly after Christmas, I went to the Greenwich Hospital for a mammogram and, after several readings, the gynecologist informed me that I had breast cancer and recommended a double mastectomy. David knew of a doctor in California who was conducting a trial, and my case fit the criteria. I had interductual carcinoma, and, according to Dr. Lagos, the biopsy had totally removed the malignancy, which had been isolated in the duct. There was no need to do anything further.

I wanted to accept this opinion and go with the trial, but my family doctor was adamant that I do "something." I had my choice of a lumpectomy and radiation or a mastectomy. My family also insisted on some treatment.

I searched for a doctor who I felt I could trust, but the ones I saw treated me like a number. I saw a well-known surgeon in New York on Park Avenue who looked at the x-rays and said, "We'll just remove the right breast. See my secretary for an appointment."

A year went by, and I had not found a doctor who would even take the time to listen to me. I then heard about a doctor at Yale in New Haven, but he was on sabbatical. I waited for him to return and knew when I met him that he was worth waiting for.

Dr. McKhan actually listened to me. He was sensitive and did not make me feel that my breast was just a useless piece of meat to be removed. We decided together to give it some thought. The lesion had been very small to begin with, and he felt we could wait. On my next visit to see Dr. McKhan, he told me that the wife of a very well-known doctor at Yale had the exact same diagnosis and was having a mastectomy. That was my decision.

Dr. McKhan arranged for me to meet a plastic surgeon who would do reconstruction directly after the surgery while I was still under anesthesia. I decided with Dr. Aryan to have the abdominal flap, in which part of the muscle from my stomach was pulled through the rib cage and placed where my breast had been. It was an intricate and painful operation, as in addition to the surgery to remove my breast, I had to be cut right across the stomach from hip to hip in order to pull the muscle through. But, as a result, I would not have anything artificial in my body.

I was so sensitive to be losing my breast and my femininity. I felt that I would never be a desirable woman again, but I had not counted on Henry, who showered me with love and tenderness. He called me a *"sshte auf mannerl."* It is a German doll. No matter how many times you push it down it comes right back up again. I think it is true. I am a *"sshte auf mannerl."*

I had the operation in May. We went to a July Fourth party and started packing to move to Vero Beach, Florida. We moved to a house I loved on Treasure Lane, September 16, 1987. I did not know how hot it could be in September in Florida. Of the three moving men, only one did not become too ill from the heat to finish the job. It was a very difficult move.

Bougainvillea by Marcy Von Kohorn

Chapter Thirty-one

My Father

My father and I remained close, but I did not confide my financial difficulties to him. Rose continued to manipulate situations to cause problems between us. Henry became like a son to Dad, but when my father named Henry as trustee in his will, Rose knew she had to break up this friendship. When she and Henry were talking on the phone, she said something rude about his mother. Rather than answering her back or expressing anger, he just hung up the phone.

After that, my father was not allowed to see or to talk to Henry, as "Henry had insulted his wife." I wrote him many letters to try to mend the relationship, but none were ever answered.

On my father's seventieth birthday, Rose had a huge and glamorous party for him. Though I had not been invited, I went and without Henry. I had not seen my father in some time, as I had not been welcome in their home, but I felt it was important, no matter what the circumstances, to be at his birthday party.

It was in Palm Beach where they had their winter house. Fortunately, my mother and Lou were in Hollywood. They had rented a condo for a short vacation. Dr. Schechter, our family doctor and friend, was also vacationing there and was invited to the party. He, of course, knew the family history. He had known me as a child.

He drove me to the party. I will always have that picture in my memory of my father standing at the top of the steps. Our eyes met, and there was a tortured message between us. I wondered if he knew the truth and just needed to have peace. Dad was handsome as always, and even though I was hurt, I loved him with my whole heart.

I wished there were some way that I could straighten out this situation that had been allowed to fester and to grow out of proportion. We had no further contact the whole evening.

Shortly after that night, my father had a stroke. My heart was broken when I saw him. At first, he was paralyzed, but that got better in time. His therapy and determination gave him back some of his strength, but he never was able to speak again. It seemed his memory was also impaired, and he had blank spots from the past. I never really knew how much he remembered, but although he asked for Henry, Rose never permitted him to see Henry again.

She now had complete charge of everything, and Dad became totally dependent on her. My father was like a magnificent tree, cut down, lying lopsided and damaged beyond repair.

The stroke came at the time we were moving out of our Pecksland Road house. The boys were older, and we only had Craig and Bob at home. Every day I would pack a box from the old house, load it in the car and drive to New York to see Dad in the hospital. I would then drive back to Greenwich, unload the box, put the things where they belonged in the new house and return home to make dinner. That was my routine for months. I needed to be with my father.

Rose and I had developed an easy, casual relationship as though nothing had happened. We had lunch together every day and never discussed the past. It was a truce. I never doubted that she loved him in her way and was hurting for him.

After that, my father's health deteriorated. He fell and broke his hip and was again in the hospital. Through the years, Dad tried to do the right thing by me. He had a best friend and golf buddy by the name of John Findley whom he confided in. John was a good person and would do anything for my father.

With John's help, my father had a codicil to his will drawn up by an attorney, which he gave to John to keep safe. The codicil expressed the wish to have his three daughters treated equally and especially to include me in his will.

Henry and I were in Florida for a brief escape from the cold weather, and John asked me to visit him in his apartment in Boca Raton. That is when he showed me this codicil. Until then, I knew nothing about it.

Although John was a decent man and a dear friend, he had a weakness. He talked too much and confided this information to a mutual friend, who then told Rose. I was accused of influencing Dad to do this, and he was then no longer allowed to see or to talk to his friend John Findley, whom he was forced to renounce.

Several years later, Rose decided to take a trip to Europe with some friends. Dad, of course, could not go. They now had a full-time housekeeper, cook and nurse by the name of Ethel. She was an excellent nurse. She slept in Dad's room and took very good care of him but reported everything to Rose.

It was summer, and they were back in Philadelphia. I wanted Dad to come visit me in Greenwich and see his grandsons. Rose gave her permission as long as Henry was not there. Before he came, I asked him by phone if he wanted Henry there. He answered yes. I could understand his words now, even though he could only make sounds. I said, "Well, we just won't tell Rose." (I forgot about Ethel.)

It was a wonderful visit. I cooked a special dinner which Dad enjoyed. It was a joy to see him and Henry together again, and he had not seen his grandchildren for many years. Afterward, I realized that Ethel would report this to Rose, so I told Dad that he had better tell her himself, which he did.

Shortly after, he had another stroke, which Rose blamed on me. When I went to visit him at the hospital, I had to be sure Rose was not there. The nurses told me that Rose was the meanest woman they had ever met.

Rose sold their homes in Philadelphia and in Palm Beach, and they moved to an apartment in West Palm Beach. It was near the Norton Museum. Rose bought two apartments and combined them to make one large and luxurious one.

When I came to see Dad now, I was not allowed to come to the apartment. I rented a car and drove around in the car with Dad and with Ethel. Sometimes, I would drive and sometimes Ethel would drive so I could sit in the back seat with Dad and have a more comfortable visit with him. He was still a handsome man, with his full head of white hair and his well-trimmed mustache. His deep brown eyes looked sad, but he always had a smile. He carried himself with dignity and was still fit and tanned from years of golfing at his beloved club where he had so many friends.

Sometimes we would walk together, holding hands and be comfortable not speaking. At times, we would meet the mailman, whom he would greet. He could make some sounds though he could not talk, but I was glad he was able to walk after his second stroke. It hurt him when he saw one of his old friends cross to the other side of the street to avoid trying to talk to him.

Once, Dad told Ethel to go to the bank. It was a drive-in, and he cashed a check for $150 and gave it to me for my plane fare. Ethel reported this to Rose who insisted that I return the money.

On all these visits, I stayed with Celia, my first mother-in-law, who had an apartment there for the winter months. She lived alone with a caretaker, as Ben had long since died. Celia and I always remained good friends, and I slept in the twin bed next to her. I loved her dearly. She always had a way of letting me know how much I meant to her.

Once, I stayed in a friend's house in Lantana. She was not there and was happy to let me use it, so I had it all to myself. It was small but comfortable. I thought how nice it would be for Dad and me to sit together. I could fix him lunch, and we could watch TV together, but Rose gave orders to Ethel that Dad was not allowed to come into that house.

In all these years, Dad and I never talked to each other about Rose. I never complained to him. I just accepted the situation as it was and did the best I could. After several years went by, when I guess she felt she had punished me enough, I was allowed to come into their apartment to visit Dad, but I still stayed with Celia or in a hotel if Celia was not yet in Florida.

Chapter Thirty-two

Rose

Rose was unhappy and bored. Her days of glamorous parties were over. Dad shared a bedroom with Ethel, and Rose remained in the master bedroom. She mostly stayed in bed, reading novels or watching TV. Every once in a while, she went out to play canasta with what few friends she had left. She was now in her seventies.

Mother called me to tell me that there was an obituary for Rose in the Philadelphia newspaper. Rose had died. Were it not for that, I would not have known. My "sisters" did not see fit to tell me.

I called my father, and Ethel answered the phone. I told Ethel that I was coming to Florida to see my father. She asked me why, since I had been there recently, and I answered, "Because my father's wife died, and I want to pay my respects to him." She then said, "Have you asked your sister's permission?" I was irate and said, "Since when do I have to ask anyone's permission to see my father? Just tell them I will be there on Thursday."

When I arrived in Palm Beach two days later and went to the Rapallo apartments, the doorman informed me that Ethel, Jackie and Susie had packed up everything and moved my father to New York.

I was so upset, I went to my hotel room and called Henry. He advised me to call Art Ivey, our family attorney. Art told me to call the police and report my father as missing. I did that.

I returned home the next day and received a call from Susie to tell me that Dad had moved into Jackie's apartment. I protested, knowing how much Dad loved his life in sunny Florida.

"Why could he not live there with Ethel to take care of him?" I asked. It was obvious that I no longer had anything to say about my father. I was told that I would be permitted to visit him every Wednesday at 1:30 in New York. I followed this schedule for many years.

On the occasion that it was not convenient for Susie to be there, my visit was canceled. I was not allowed to be alone with him, and if I was briefly, it was obvious that everything I said was being monitored.

Once in a while, I would show him a paper, maybe something from one of the children. Once an article appeared in the newspaper about Henry. Quickly Jackie or Susie would appear to see what I was showing him. I did not get it! Jackie was usually in a worn terry robe and made no attempt to be cordial. Susie was a little friendlier.

Dad tried to communicate with me. There were some words I could understand. He would take my hand and kiss it and say, "I love you." Sometimes, he would cry. I would say, "Don't cry, Daddy. I'm here to make you happy and because I love you."

I would call him every Sunday at 6 o'clock. I think he looked forward to those calls even though it was a one-way conversation, except for a few words I was able to make out. Wherever I was on Sunday, I found a way to call him, even if I had to find a pay phone.

Many times, toward the end when I was there, he refused to eat. Ethel was still with him for a short time. She told me that Rose had died while she was on the phone with her sister, whom she was suing at the time. Ethel was fired, and they had a new and strange nurse there every time. One time, I thought my father tried to say "poison" when the nurse or Jackie forced his mouth open and put food in it. I had to look away. It was so cruel, and I wondered what he was trying to tell me.

When Rose was alive, she tried to break the bond between us. I loved him very much. I was willing to jump through hoops of fire to be with him. And that I did!

Chapter Thirty-three

My Father's Will

On November 6, 1984, I was baking a birthday cake for Craig. I was expecting the family for dinner, to celebrate. I received a call from Susie. She insisted that I come at once to see Dad. She said the doctor wanted to take Dad to the hospital for observation, and he did not want to go. I asked her if he was sick. She answered, "No, he is sitting up in bed, drinking a chocolate soda."

I wondered that all of a sudden they wanted my opinion. It was a Tuesday, and I reminded her that I would be there tomorrow, as usual, and whatever the problem was, we could talk about it then. She said that Dad wanted to make the decision now, and he wanted his three girls to talk about it.

She was so insistent that I waited ten minutes to take the cake out of the oven, and I left a note to the family to have Craig's birthday dinner without me. When I arrived in New York and saw the ambulance, I knew it was Dad.

I rushed upstairs where my father was lying on the floor. He was dead.

I screamed at Susie and Jackie, "Get out of this room!" They had never seen me so angry, and they both looked frightened. They got out, and finally I was alone with my father. Dad was eighty-four years old.

I cried and held him in my arms to say goodbye to him. When I opened the door, ready to leave for home, amazingly, they were concerned for me that I should not be driving, and they persuaded me to call Henry to come take me home, as I was in no condition to drive.

The police were called. They wanted to do an autopsy, but Jackie was adamant, and she produced a letter from a doctor not to permit an autopsy.

Henry drove there to pick me up.

I must confess I had never thought much about Dad's will. I knew from what had happened with John Findley that he wanted his estate to be divided equally. In everything my father did, he was fair. He was a "man of all seasons." He had no bigotry. He got along with everyone.

When Marion Anderson, the famous opera singer, wanted to make a reservation at the Warwick Hotel, because she was a woman of color, the Board decided not to accept her reservation. I don't think I ever saw my father so angry. Even though he owned the hotel, the Board was important. I do not know how he was able to change the vote, but Marion Anderson stayed at the Warwick Hotel. Many famous people stayed there, including President and Mrs. Roosevelt.

I vaguely remember Dad's funeral, but I do remember that John Findley was there. I wrote a poem which I spoke from the pulpit. It said, "We are here to say goodbye." Susie also said something, but Jackie did not. It was the last time we were ever together as friends.

Shortly after, I received the will. Henry opened it and saw the codicil at once and that it was not signed by Dad. It was Rose's handwriting. I was left $35,000 if I did not contest the will. My uncle Leonard (Mother's brother) was an attorney and was able to find a Philadelphia law firm that would accept the case on contingency. The strange words of long ago came back to me. "I will get my revenge on you, if I have to come back from the grave to do it." I was so torn apart to think that my father did not love me enough to leave me anything. When we examined the pages, we found that the ink on the codicil was different, as well as the signature. My father's secretary, Ethel Duben, testified that Rose had her type up the codicil. Clarence, the chauffer, said that he drove her to the lawyer's office where the codicil was added to the will.

So much of the proceeding, I do not remember. It took place in Palm Beach. Henry was with me, but he was not permitted to come inside. We did not think it would take more than a day, so we did not make a hotel reservation anywhere.

We sat around a large oval conference table with my two attorneys on one side and Jackie and Susie on the other side with their attorney. It was as if I were on trial. "Isn't it true that your father paid for you to go to camp?" I answered, "Yes." "Isn't it true that your father paid for you to go to Edgewood Park? "Yes."

Many times during this inquisition, Jackie would lean over to whisper something to her lawyer, but my attorneys never objected to any questions. It was obvious that he was well prepared. My attorneys sat there and really were useless.

I do not remember any questions from them about possible forgery. I now learned why I was not allowed to be alone with Dad. The girls were afraid that I would bring him a will to sign, leaving everything to me. That was the reason they could not permit him to go to the hospital, because they could not control when I visited him at the hospital.

This all came out at this meeting. They certainly gave me credit for being much smarter than I am, but it never even entered my mind. If anything, I would have respected Dad's wishes. One of my attorneys seemed totally disinterested, but the other lawyer, Abe, was very caring. They were both unprepared.

Much of this day has either been forgotten or buried deep inside my subconscious. At the end of the session, I had to return the following day. Henry and I had no place to stay in Palm Beach, and it was impossible to find a hotel room during season. The place where we ended up staying must have been for call girls. The pay phone rang all night, and it was just outside our room.

We did not get much sleep, but I was so distraught that I would not have slept anyhow. We met again the next day when their attorney produced statements from three Florida lawyers testifying that Dad was taken to their office where he confirmed the forged will. My attorneys packed up their brief cases and left, but not before one of them said, "Accept it, your father did not wish to give you anything in his will."

It is possible that those statements were bought and paid for, but who knows, maybe my father was forced or threatened. I always wondered why they did not produce those statements the first day. It was the end of any relationship I had with my two step sisters.

I had a dear friend by the name of Lily Howell, who lived across the street on Pecksland Road. Henry and I spent a lot of wonderful evenings with Lily and John, and our children played together. Their oldest daughter Kelly and I were close. Kelly had an interest in the paranormal and, when Dad died, she gave me as a gift a reading with a psychic named Marcie Seidel.

I didn't really believe in psychics, but I went to please Kelly. At that session Marcie claimed to see Dad in his golf knickers. (He always wore knickers for golf.) She said that he was trying to tell me something, that he was breaking a packet of powder over his food. We finally understood that he wanted me to know that he had been poisoned.

I later found out that Marcie Seidel was well known and was often asked to help solve cases with the police department. Who knows? I remembered the way he tried to push his food away. Anything was possible.

In some strange way, though I missed him, it was a relief not to have to deal with the stress I had to face in order to be with my father. With it all, I never stopped loving him. Mother and I did not talk about him much, but I knew it was hard for her also.

When Dad died, she had an angina attack and was sent to the hospital. In my life, I never had a better friend than my Mom. She gave me unconditional love, but I knew she had an unhappy life. She never stopped loving my father, and Lou was not easy to live with. He cursed at her and ordered her around like a servant.

Chapter Thirty-four

Move to Florida

We had a big party for Mother on her ninetieth birthday at her favorite restaurant. We rented a private room. All my uncles, whom I loved so much, were there with their wives. My favorite, Uncle Danny, was crippled with a disintegrating spine. Uncle Leonard was there. He was a lawyer, and Mother's youngest brother Otzy, who was still fit from his weightlifting days, and also Lou, who was happy to be with the family.

Mother's Ninetieth Birthday Party

Every one of my sons, my daughters-in-law, and my grandchildren, and even Melissa, Meredith's sister, were there to honor my darling mother. Craig and Kathy decorated the Coastline restaurant with an eight-foot banner that David had made. There were place cards and loads of balloons. Mother was thrilled and proud of her family.

Then Henry and all the boys got together for a photo (above). It was such a wonderful day, I could not stop crying.

I stayed on with Mother for a few more days. When I left her, I always left part of my heart behind. I knew she was getting older and dreaded the day I would lose her.

It was hard for Mother and me when Henry and I decided to move to Florida. It was also hard to move away from the boys and my grandchildren. I would miss seeing them grow up. We still visited Mother often and never missed the family Christmas party every year, usually held at Henry and Meredith's house. Craig and Kathy moved to Vero Beach, and it was so good that we had family nearby. When Kyle and Courtney were born, Henry and I were part of their growing up years.

Every Monday baby Kyle spent the day with us. I took him to the beach and then home for a lamb chop and baked potato in his high chair for lunch. Grandpa and I played music and danced for him. Then he went down for his nap.

When they were a little older, I picked them up at the Osceola School, and we went across the street for gelato and water ice. I took Kyle to karate and Courtney to singing lessons, and every Wednesday, I took them to tennis lessons at the Moorings Club. Henry played pool with Kyle on the pool table downstairs in our condo and always had some original way to challenge their minds. They loved their Grandpa.

Kyle and Courtney

It is said that "it takes a village to raise a child" and we were part of that village.

Marcy & Henry with grandchildren

~

My art was still an important part of my life. It was an escape for me, and when I was painting, I forgot every care in the world. The trouble was, once I started painting, I never wanted to stop.

I still went to Greenwich Village for lessons every Monday with Catherine and Louise. I had been juried into the well-known Catharine Lorillard Wolfe Art Club. I became a member of the Board and was Chairperson of the 101st Preview Reception held at the National Art Club on Gramercy Park South in New York City.

My friend, Olga Hirshhorn, was prominent on the invitation as an honorary chairperson. Joe Hirshhorn had donated his collection to the Hirshhorn Museum next to the Smithsonian in Washington, D.C. I was pictured handing a donation from the Catharine Lorillard Wolfe Club to Philippe de Montebello, president of the Metropolitan Museum.

In 1981, Miss Kan's class had an exhibition at the Elliott Museum in Stuart, Florida. I had entered a painting of "Forsythia" in the crinkle technique. The show was written up in the local newspaper with a small paragraph about my painting, saying, "The painting that was most to be treasured was the Sunny Forsythia by Marcy Von Kohorn."

Sunny Forsythia by Marcy Von Kohorn

140

As a result of this special mention, I was invited to have a one person show at the Elliott Museum in 1985. That is how Henry and I discovered Vero Beach, and in 1987 we moved there.

I was invited to have another show in 2005 at the Elliott Museum Each time was a great honor for me, and I could not believe the huge attendance.

In Vero Beach, I was one of the founding members of the Artist Guild. In 1994, I joined the Rablen West Gallery and showed there for about ten years, until the gallery went out of business. I won many prizes, the most important being first prize at a show at the Norton Museum and also a prize at a show at Lincoln Center in New York City.

My paintings are now hanging on many walls. It makes me feel as though I am sharing a beauty that lives within me. I am very grateful for that gift.

Majestic Mountains by Marcy Von Kohorn

Chapter Thirty-five

Candelaria

Henry came home one day and told me he bought a silver mine in Tonopah, Nevada for $18,000. The mine was called Candeleria, and it turned out to be very lucrative. It had become too dangerous to work the mine underground, so it had been closed down for a long time.

It had been worked by cheap Chinese labor. There were old Chinese newspapers, coins and artifacts that were left by the Chinese who had labored there.

Henry and I went to see many different companies to try to find investors. We went to Superior Oil, Homestead, and several smaller companies in Colorado. We finally got a deal with Armand Hammer of Occidental Petroleum.

We had a joint venture. They supplied all the heavy equipment and expertise. Aside from silver, there was high-grade gold. It was at the time that the Hunt brothers drove the price of silver up to twenty dollars an ounce. Armand Hammer sold silver short and made around ninety million dollars.

If he had lost in the market, he was prepared to deliver the silver from the mine. For that reason, he made the investment in the name of Candeleria Industries. When we asked for our share of the profits, Hammer refused to recognize the partnership, so we hired a prestigious law firm on contingency.

We had seven attorneys over a period of seven years working on the case. Occidental Petroleum had their own "in house" law firm.

Even with the important firm we worked with, we were still up against big guns.

The trial took place in Reno, Nevada. Armand Hammer arrived in his own private helicopter. He was eighty-eight years old and bristled with his own sense of importance.

Hammer had many ties to the Soviet Union. He did business there and had many interests and business associates there. It was during the time of the "cold war" and some Americans built bomb shelters in fear of an attack by the Soviet Union. The average American feared Stalin and communism.

During the deposition, Hammer answered every question with "I don't know" or "I don't remember." He did the same in front of the jury.

It's hard to say what triggered the sudden talking spree when Hammer praised the Soviet Union and told of his many connections there.

It was not exactly what an unsophisticated, small town jury wanted to hear and had nothing to do with the case. The jury awarded us a great deal of money, most of which went to the lawyers. Because Hammer thought we might appeal the case for a larger amount, he offered us a settlement and bought out our share of the mine.

Patents

In the eighties and before anyone knew about computers, Henry talked to me about "interactive television." He was convinced that there would be a way for people to communicate on the television and began to take out patents. The patents were expensive, but the patent attorneys did a good job for him.

Later in life Henry was able to write his own patents. The claims were very broad and therefore there was great leeway in their interpretation. When computers became a part of every household, one was able to print out coupons which became a lucrative business.

Response Reward Systems, of which Henry was president, was a Florida company that was formed to hold Henry's patents and through which we sued many companies for infringement. Some companies recognized that they were infringing and paid the fee to become licensees, but with most, we had to sue. We had to hire a patent attorney to advise us and to write legal complaints to the court. The lawsuits were very stressful and most dragged on, sometimes for years, but we always ended up with a settlement and never had to go to court.

There were times, as part of the process, when the patents had to be reexamined, but not one was ever invalidated. Jamie, the Intellectual Property attorney who represented Sony, was the only one who was not hostile. Jamie and Henry became friends and later worked together.

In all, Henry had fifty-six patents, many on machinery for VKIC and seventeen on the internet.

Henry kept taking out patents, and money became an issue, as patents were very expensive. No doubt, between patent applications and patent attorneys, maintenance fees and suing infringers, we must have spent millions. (I was in charge of the banking. I guess I was the CFO!)

The patents became a big part of our lives. In the beginning, Henry became involved with a company called Legend Central owned by Jim and Robert Ryan. In September of 1993, after many phone conversations and meetings with Jim in New York, Jim sent Henry a plane ticket to go to Los Angeles, California, to meet with him and his father, Robert, to discuss a deal to buy his internet patents.

The first night he was there and invited for dinner, Henry described a very bizarre dinner party. Jim was not married and lived in this mansion with his father, who was also not married. Murdoch and Liz Taylor were neighbors. No liquor was served, and when Henry asked for a drink, they sent to the cellar for a bottle.

Henry ended up staying in their Bell Air home for a week. He said it looked like a Hollywood movie set and described total opulence. There was a large pool, a pool house and lots of pretty girls, a guesthouse and lots of servants. There was a fax in every room and about twelve telephones.

145

They were planning on working on a contract over the weekend. When Henry returned, he brought a lot of literature about Legend Central, which I spent a long time reading. It was impressive and looked like a perfect fit with Response Reward Systems, especially because their system was locked into couponing. I was thinking that they needed our patents or a license in order to proceed.

They were trying to raise enough money for an option to buy the couponing patents. The industry was growing quickly now that computers were being developed. It was creating a new lifestyle.

There was a story in the Wall Street Journal that Hewlitt Packard and Time Warner were going to do couponing. Another trail for Henry to follow up. The New York Times carried a story that Bell South bought Liberty Media for thirty-one million.

Meanwhile Henry was working on another patent with 267 claims. He ended up with seventeen patents on the internet, most of them about couponing. His other patents included the Rescue Pad, the Nylonge Sponge, line calls in tennis, separating cyanide from ore in mining, Moodlite, and an insect repellant. He also had an editing patent (for parental control). He was way ahead of his time!

Even with all the time and energy spent on the patents, I painted whenever I could. I could no longer attend the classes in New York, but Miss Kan gave a three-week workshop in October in Panama City, Florida, and Henry went there with me.

Aside from Vero Beach, my paintings were in galleries in Stuart, Palm Beach, Winter Park and Orlando. My paintings were selling. I had to check periodically as sometime when a painting sold, the gallery owner never told me. Amazing! There was life outside the patents!

Jim of Legend Central continued with their efforts to make some kind of a deal, which always fell through at the last minute. Henry met with Legend Central lawyers in New York to find underwriters. They had an option until January 1994, which was then extended another month for $50,000. Meanwhile, I was counting my pennies and not able to pay bills. I wondered if Jim had any intentions of putting up the money, or if he was just stringing us along.

Henry kept going back and forth to New York to negotiate a contract with Jim, and finally took an apartment at the Yale Club. I missed him, and when he returned home, his flight was canceled because of bad weather. He was then rerouted to Baltimore, then Atlanta. When he finally landed in Melbourne, Florida, he looked so tired and was limping badly.

I was glad to have him home and to be able to reach over at night and know he was next to me.

They never did have a deal.

It did not take long for Henry to be working again in the contour chair, nor did it take long for life to get back to normal. "Quiet, Marcy, I'm a working!" And normal, too, Jim missed the promised deadline for another payment.

Henry had a great serve.

Chapter Thirty-six

Hip Surgery

Henry loved his tennis and continued to play in tournaments, improving his national ranking. As a senior he was ranked #1 in New England. At one point he began to have problems with his hip. The specialist in Vero said his hip was worn down and that he had a degenerated disc.

The specialist agreed to do the operation but said that Henry would never play singles again. That, of course, was not acceptable!

Our dear friend, Harry Hopman, who was the famous Australian Davis Cup coach had a double hip operation and was back on the courts. Dr. Ranawat at the Hospital for Special Surgery in New York had operated on him.

I arranged to rent an apartment in Sutton Place in Manhattan for six weeks. The apartment belonged to the son of my good friend, Joan Lowther. I made arrangements with Dr. Ranawat's secretary, as I wanted Henry to donate blood in case he would need a blood transfusion. It turned out that he did need one, and it was much safer to have his own blood. I confirmed the dates of March 9 for blood work, March 10 for pre-admission tests and March 15 for surgery

We left Vero Beach on March 7, Kyle's birthday. Craig drove us to the airport. I felt a tug at my heart to leave home and at what we had ahead of us. The plane trip was fine, and we were lucky to have had help with our bags, but on our way to stay at Ken's, we realized that Henry had left his briefcase in the men's room at the airport. (Memories of Abu Dhabi when we visited Wahib.)

We went back to get the briefcase, and I found a shiny penny in the airport, just like the one my grandfather Morris used to give me, and thought it was a good omen.

The next day I changed my mind about the penny. It was the day that we were in the hospital for Henry to donate blood for himself. All went well, and we went to the little restaurant across the street for lunch. Henry had corned beef and cabbage and two beers.

Shortly after, while we were still at the restaurant, Henry said he felt weak. With that his head rolled forward, his eyes in a glassy stare. He did not see me or hear me. His mouth was turned down, and I thought he was having a stroke. I shouted for someone to call 911. It lasted for a few seconds. Then he scolded me for waking him up. He said he just wanted to sleep and kept sliding in and out of consciousness.

It seemed like an eternity until the medics arrived. They took him into the ambulance. I was so frightened. In the ambulance they gave him oxygen and an IV of fluid and took us to the emergency room. Even though the hospital was just across the street, it was a one-way street, and traffic was heavy, so we needed to go all the way around the corner.

At the emergency room they would not permit me to be with him. I had to wait outside. I was shaking and sobbing so much that the black guard on duty took pity on me and requested the social worker to come talk to me.

Finally, the nurse came out to tell me Henry was fine and allowed me to be with him while they checked on his blood test results. They discharged him, and we walked about a half a block to see Dr. Perrone with whom we had an appointment. We were a little late. He did an ultrasound of Henry's heart, and all was well. He said the attack he suffered was because of the two beers after having given blood.

The next day Henry was angry at me because I told the family what had happened. It would have been impossible for me to go through such a traumatic experience without sharing it with the family, but Henry had this stoic side to him. I was never to discuss anything personal.

He did not ever talk to the boys about anything personal, and they often complained about his lack of warmth. I guess I was the only one he allowed to know the part of him he kept so hidden.

Dr. Ranawat operated on Henry five days later. I was nervous, but everything went well. It helped that Bob was with me. I was able to stay with Henry on a cot in his room that night. Bob said that the brothers got together to take turns to be with me.

Two days later Henry was walking with a walker, and five days later we were on our way to the apartment we rented.

While Henry was in the hospital, I walked to Woolworths for the things he would need like extra pillows which the doctor requested. I also purchased cooking utensils and pots and pans as the kitchen was not well stocked. It was a short walk though from our apartment to Gristedes, the wonderful super market which delivered. That was important as my foot was hurting.

I ended up seeing Dr. Bohne at the hospital who diagnosed me with a stress fracture. He said I had broken the bone about ten days ago (maybe carrying the four pillows). He gave me a surgical boot to wear. It sure was ugly but helped a lot. Several days later I went back to the hospital for a bone scan and to be evaluated for osteoporosis. I did have osteoporosis but not too bad. I also went to Lincoln Center to see my painting which was accepted by the National League of American Pen Women, of which I was a member. I won first prize for my painting Serenity.

Serenity by Marcy Von Kohorn

It is always a thrill to see my paintings hanging anywhere, but Lincoln Center was pretty special. I had my paints in the apartment and was painting a little every day. There was a flower stand outside the building. I liked to paint from nature, and there were flowers that did not grow in Florida that inspired me.

When Henry was recuperating, we often had visits from Jim. He would make an appointment to see us in the morning and would show up in the afternoon. He and his friend Jack often stayed for dinner. I did not mind because it was stimulating for Henry to talk about his patents.

There were promises of payments by April first and a false report of a deposit put in the Union Trust Bank account. He and Henry decided that they would keep the patent assignment in escrow, and Henry would turn them over on receipt of all the money. The following day, Robert called to say that we would have the money by the end of April and nine million shortly after that.

The day before we left New York to go back to Florida, we met at the City Corp Private Bank to open an escrow account so we would be ready to receive the money and to put the patent assignment in. The patents were to be turned over when ten million was paid.

The five weeks we spent in New York had been very special. We had wonderful visits from the family and our Connecticut friends and, most important, got to see our grandchildren.

Easter Sunday, Bob and Dana spent the day with us, and I hid the colored eggs for Olivia and Melody downstairs in the garden.

Henry and I took walks together, and for the first time ever, he went to the market with me. He improved every day and, by the time we left for home, he was totally pain free.

Chapter Thirty-seven

Patent Problems

One night, several months later, I received a phone call from a man who told me that Jim was showing legal papers to clients to prove that he owned the Von Kohorn patents. The papers had Henry's forged signature. He said that if Henry accepted any money from him, Jim, it could tie him up with lawsuits and prevent us from making any other deals.

He also pleaded with me not to divulge his name, claiming that he feared for his life and that of his wife and children. Henry was not concerned. I was.

I also had a call from a man who wanted to know if Legend Central owned the Von Kohorn patents.

I was upset. Henry was not going to pay any attention to these warnings. Was there something I did not know? I called our attorney, who called Legend Central's lawyers. Their lawyers told Richard that they were "wise to them and that they have been making misrepresentations about their firm, too."

In those days, whenever Henry had a lead, he traveled to make a presentation. He was relentless!

At one point he called me from New York, elated with the news that he had a deal with Time Warner. Although he did not have the figures yet, they were sending us a proposal. When he arrived home again, he looked so tired, but happy.

How sweet my life was when it wasn't interrupted by events beyond my control. We were running out of money. Henry was so confident about RRS that he did not worry about money and kept on spending on patents.

The Time Warner deal fell through, too.

We had a proposal from an attorney by the name of Manuel who was willing to work on contingency to sue infringers. He was a Harvard graduate and did not want any expenses until we had made $250,000. We discovered that he had an unsavory reputation and had left his wife and children penniless.

After many encouraging meetings that Henry and I went to with ABC and CBS, Bell Atlantic and IBM, trying to do joint ventures or to sell the patents that all fell through, we decided the way to go was to sue infringers.

I often wondered if all those companies who seemed so interested did their homework and turned us down because we had been dealing with Jim and Robert Ryan. Their name connected to RRS could have put a cloud on the patents.

Local Inventor Strikes Again

Von Kohorn, 84, Develops
Patented Interactive Systems

"I was ahead of the mindset of people. It's only been in the last few years that executives, primarily in television, have come to realize this type of entertainment and direct marketing is desirable and profitable. Before that, they couldn't see beyond their noses."

Henry Von Kohorn as told to Chris Kauffmann, Staff Writer, Vero Beach Press Journal

While Henry held 56 patents, 17 were in the areas of interactive entertainment and direct-response marketing.

Chapter Thirty-eight

Health Problems

In 1995, we spoke to a patent attorney who was willing to represent us. And so began our relationship with David Flint.

When we first met David at his office in Stamford, Connecticut, he told us story after story about his successful legal battles. He told us that he had sued one hundred and fifty cases at one time.

Two days later, we signed a contract with him. He was very impressed with Henry's patents and claims.

About three months later, we filed our first suit in the White Plains courthouse against AT&T. David, Henry and I spent hours discussing a proper press release. Catalina Marketing was also infringing. We filed a complaint against them in June.

Flint seemed to have great confidence in the patents. He was willing to go to battle for us. He found twenty-five coupon sites on the Web through Yahoo.

Henry was now eighty-three, and the years of stress were beginning to show. He complained on and off about chest pains, and his blood pressure was high.

I also was having health issues. I would feel faint and was close to passing out. I would then break out in a cold sweat and had bad headaches.

I was learning that winning infringement suits was a slow process. There is a patent analysis, discovery, negotiations, all to avoid going to court. AT&T, David and Henry and I had a meeting with their attorney and several of their executives. When Henry made a presentation to them, he was impressive, but because of the structure of the company, it was not clear whether or not they were infringing.

On the same trip north, we met with Time Warner. They were quite surprised that we had sued AT&T. They asked whether we had a "legal opinion" on our patents. Henry said no, that it would be very costly to obtain one. We discussed what would be an appropriate settlement, and they agreed to get back to us after studying the patents. We also met with Froehlich of E-Data.

Henry always referred to me as his partner. He even gave me a beautiful gold disc for my charm bracelet which was engraved "to my partner."

Shortly after, we filed a complaint against Catalina. He and David sent out dozens of letters and faxes, enjoying the publicity.

The name Response Reward Systems (RRS) was definitely out there by now.

In 1996, we ended up receiving a royalty from Catalina for $25,000 a year. We received $40,000 a year from Valpak, who did not dispute that they were infringing, and other small royalties in addition to paid-up licenses.

Our legal expenses were still high, between maintenance fees and bills from Perman & Green, the patent attorney who wrote the patents. Part of each payment to us went to Flint. It was a big relief, though, to finally have an income, but the stress was difficult.

In October Henry had a TIA in which he had temporary symptoms of a stroke that lasted several hours. I knew that a TIA was a warning.

Our cardiologist, Dr. Cho, was wonderful, but she could only do so much and said that his heart muscle was weak and not pumping blood adequately. She did assure me that his condition was treatable and kept him in the hospital for observation. He seemed to be improving.

A few days later, I noticed that he was not himself. He was lethargic and wanted to sleep all the time. His nurse told me that during the night he tried to get up to go to the bathroom, and his knees buckled, and he fell. During the day I noticed a slight impairment, and he complained about his vision. I asked Craig and Kathy to come to the hospital to confirm my opinion. They saw it, too.

When I was getting ready to leave the hospital that day and told the floor nurse I was leaving, she said, "I'm sorry about the seizure he had last night."

Linda, his nurse said, "That was not a seizure; he had a small stroke."

I spoke to Dr. Cho. She said, "Don't you think, if that were true, it would have been reported to me?"

I knew something had happened to Henry and felt my world had come to an end. He was my world!

There was such a change in him. I called the neurologist, Dr. Miranda, to come see him.

He finally came at about 6 o'clock and said that Henry had had a "completed stroke." Part of his vision was impaired, and his left side was very weak. When the doctor got him to stand, Henry fell right into his arms. Dr. Cho outlined her suggested treatment for him. She would do a cat scan and, when he was strong enough, send him to Health South for rehabilitation.

She told me that she had read the report of the doctor on duty that night which read that Henry had flailed and lost consciousness. Dr. Cho was wonderful.

When I arrived at the hospital the next day and saw his nurse put him in a chair at the basin with a pan of cold water and razor in his hand and say, "Wash and shave," I was livid. I'm glad I was there to do it for him.

I also made it a point to be there at meal times. An aide would come in and put a tray of food in front of him. Henry was unable to unwrap the utensils or even to hold them. If he had not touched his food, the tray was removed.

Another day when I arrived in the morning, Henry told me that a nurse had come into his room at three a.m., awakened him and insisted that he walk. He said he lay down on the floor and refused to budge until she allowed him to go back to bed. The next day Henry's nurse was not in his room all day and was nowhere on the floor.

Henry seemed lethargic and wanted to sleep all day. I called Dr. Cho, and she ordered an injection for him to increase his blood thinner medication. That was the first and only time I saw his nurse all day.

The injection seemed to help, and he "came to life," got up and started walking in place.

He had no appetite. I tried to bring some of his favorite foods from home. The nurses were rude to me and kept telling me to go out and have lunch with my friends and to stop "mothering" him.

He was slowly regaining his strength and teaching himself to read again. He was even working on a new patent.

Henry was moved to Health South for rehabilitation. His bed was right next to the window. It was cheerful, sunny and looked out on the green lawn. It was a good facility and cleaner than the hospital. He did have a roommate, who seemed like a decent, quiet man.

Our son Henry came, and between him, Craig, and Kathy, I felt that I was not carrying this burden alone. When Henry wanted to shave, Henry Jr. went out to buy him an electric razor because he was on a blood thinner. It meant so much to both of us to have our children around and, in time, each of them came to see their Dad. Even our grandchildren, Kyle and Courtney, came to put a smile on his face, and Ralph and Jill came from Hawaii where they were on vacation. It was such a help to me and to Henry, too, to have all this support.

Two years later, his brother Ralph had a stroke. I could feel for Jill as she cared for him. Ralph was never able to walk again.

I was there for every meal. Henry was dressed, and we ate on the porch together. I helped him, as he was still handicapped.

Little by little, thanks to the therapist and the caring staff, Henry was regaining his strength.

While he was recuperating, we received a Fed Ex from ValPak, saying that even though they were not infringing, they would like to talk about a proposal. That was a big one and helped to cheer us both up.

It was strenuous for Henry. He had occupational therapy, physical therapy and speech therapy. They worked him hard, and I felt he needed more rest.

In time I saw the improvement that I prayed for, and Henry was able to come home. He continued his therapy as an outpatient.

His vision had been damaged in his left eye. We saw a neuro ophthalmologist in Port St. Lucie. He offered us no hope. Instead he suggested special eyeglasses.

We went to Palm Beach to see an optometrist who specialized in correcting vision with prisms. The eye doctor put Henry through a grueling three-hour examination. The doctor was about to try the prisms in Henry's eyeglasses when Henry suddenly had a problem breathing.

The doctor called 911, and we were taken by ambulance to the emergency room of the Good Samaritan Hospital. We were lucky the ER doctor was a top cardiologist. He did an EKG, blood work, and a chest X-ray. By the time they checked him out and found him okay it was 10 o'clock. The kind nurses found us some sandwiches, Henry was put in a private room, and they found a cot for me.

The next morning the doctor took blood and found him well enough to be discharged. We went right to Dr. Cho, who also checked him, and we made a decision to go to the Mayo Clinic for further treatment.

Gradually, Henry recovered his strength, and Dr. Cho gave him permission to hit some balls on the ball boy machine. That was the best medicine she could have given him. He had been through so much. My heart ached for him, but I knew he was on his way to recovery. He was even able to play tennis again.

Hawaii Hibiscus by Marcy Von Kohorn

Chapter Thirty-nine

My Busy Life

It had been a busy year for me. I had been driving Henry everywhere as he was still unable to drive. He had therapy every Monday, Wednesday and Friday. While he was at therapy, I would pick Kyle up and take him to his karate class, and I took the children to Sunday school every Sunday morning. On Wednesdays, I picked them up at school and took them to tennis lessons.

I was totally in charge of the books. I paid household bills, attorneys, and all RRS expenses. I also managed all the emails that came in and were sent, as with all Henry's brilliance, he would not go near the computer.

April 2, 1996, Henry and I celebrated our 40th wedding anniversary and renewed our vows in a church wedding. Mother gave me her diamond wedding band.

Henry was still not strong enough to travel, so we could not go to the family Christmas party. I missed my darling mother so much. We made plans for her to come to us for Christmas. We even talked about having a party, but Henry had a long way to go to recover. I doubted that he would ever be completely normal again. He was still weak. It broke my heart to see him that way.

To have my Mother there with her love and her wisdom gave me the strength to go on. She was my Christmas gift, to have her part of my everyday life.

We had Christmas Eve at Craig and Kathy's with their lavishly decorated tree that reached to the ceiling. Kyle was six years old and

Kyle at Karate Class

Courtney was two. They were excited to see what Santa would leave them on Christmas morning and left cookies on the fireplace for him and carrots for the reindeer. Kathy prepared an elegant and delicious Christmas Eve dinner, and the table was beautiful.

Henry seemed better, and my Christmas prayer was to have these two dear people to share Christmas with again next year.

It was a good ending to 1996. Craig and Kathy came with the children. Henry was getting stronger, and we all took a long walk on the beach together.

Henry and I spent New Year's Eve with our friends Maggie and Glenn Johnston, as we had every year.

We even had good news from David Flint about Response Reward. We received $400,000 from Interact, and even though we had many debts to pay, I was not struggling to make ends meet. Interact approached us to buy some of the patents as they were suing Catalina.

The grandchildren were a great joy for us. Isabelle, Emily, and Dan came to see us. We were very blessed.

It was a year later that Henry passed his driver's test and could drive. He had come a long way. He had an EEG that showed a large black area in his brain and an erratic brain pattern. It was impressive that with this damage he was able to regain his mental functions. He was able to read as passionately as he used to. He wrote new patents and conducted business again. He developed an interest in astronomy and was able to grasp complicated scientific theories.

Dr. Cho said something very surprising to me. She said that I had been so supportive that I probably saved Henry's life. His life was my life.

In 1997, life resumed some normalcy. I was able to paint again and won two prestigious prizes.

We visited with Mother and celebrated her ninetieth birthday with her and once again were able to be in Connecticut for our family Christmas party. We had a big party for our friends and called it a party to celebrate that Henry was well.

Marcy Displays her Art

Chapter Forty

My Dearest Mother

I went to see Mother every couple of months, and of course we spoke on the phone almost every day. Mother was living in Cherry Hill, New Jersey in the Towers of Windsor Park. Mother was well except for a few problems. She did have angina.

Mother also had a bladder problem. I went to be with her for a urinary procedure. Lou and I took her to the hospital at six in the morning. When she was discharged, the written instructions said she should be off her feet for twenty-four hours; I tried to do everything I could to keep her comfortable.

Lou and I went to the super market to pick up a barbecued chicken and cole slaw. I helped Mother to the table. When Lou tasted the chicken, he complained that it was not hot enough. "Ceal," he said, "this is not edible. Heat it up." I would not allow Mother to get out of her chair, so I heated the chicken and tried to keep Lou happy, which was not easy.

Lou was always overweight, and as he got older, he had trouble with his circulation and also had trouble walking. He had many health issues, and in his eighties, he had a stroke. He was sent from the hospital to a rehabilitation facility in Voorhees. Mother did not drive, and it was hard for her to go back and forth to visit him.

The Towers of Windsor Park was getting shabby, so I persuaded Mother to move to a retirement home not too far from where Lou was. Lou became worse, and he was a very grumpy patient. He was sent back to the hospital where he died on December 29, 1990. He left everything to Mother and specified that on her death everything should go to me. He did have a son and a daughter, but they had no relationship.

In December of 1993, Mother and I went on a wonderful cruise together. It was a Christmas gift from Henry. We also went on a trip to Europe, a birthday gift for Mom from Henry.

In Paris we were giggling late into the night. The man next door made a complaint about us. Mother and I were like two school girls together. She was such a good sport. I wanted to show her everything, and when she begged to rest a little, I told her she could rest when she got home.

When Mother was ninety, she had breast cancer. She had a lumpectomy and then radiation. I was with her for every treatment, and she was wonderful.

After each session, when I suggested that she go home and rest, she would insist we go to lunch at Ponzio's and then do some shopping at one of the department stores. She had so much energy!

I never told Mother about my breast cancer, but I did have occasion to talk to her doctor about my decision to have a mastectomy. The doctor told me that the new thinking in the medical world is that with *intraductal insitu* carcinoma, they now do nothing after the biopsy, as the lesion has been removed.

So, Dr Lagos was right, and there was no need to have had a mastectomy. I must learn not to look back. What is done is done!

By then Mother had made friends at Brendenwood, and at least being there made it easier for her. My darling uncles had died, so mother had none of her family left.

She had an apartment on the second floor and could watch all the comings and goings from her window in the den. It was a lovely, comfortable apartment, and Mother was happy there. She had many friends and enjoyed her final years there.

One of her friends with whom she had dinner every night was a gentleman by the name of Marty. She and Marty became very close, and every night Mother would meet him at the elevator to tie his shoelaces and straighten his tie.

She also had a good friend named Ethel, who was in a wheel chair. Mother wheeled her to the table every night. One night Ethel lost her footing trying to go from the wheelchair to the dining room chair. Mother tried to catch her, and they both landed on the floor. Mother told me that she had a big lump on the back of her head. I think that was when it started!

In March, Mother called me to tell me that President Clinton was sending her diamond earrings. Awhile later she called in tears to tell me that President Clinton had been assassinated. I told her not to tell her friends until I checked it out. I called her back to tell her that President Clinton was fine. There was a long pause on the phone.

She then called with the news that her friend Polly Hunt had died and had left her a million dollars. Polly was alive and well. Her final fantasy was that Marty had proposed marriage. She wanted to know whether I thought she should marry him. I told her that they should just remain friends and not to discuss it with him as she would hurt his feelings. She did not listen to me and called him into her apartment to decide when they would get married. From that time on, Marty no longer spoke to her and refused to eat at her table.

I had gone along with her as much as I could, but Yvonne, the Director of Brendenwood, called me to complain about her. She said, "This is unacceptable behavior, and we cannot put up with it." When I talked to Mother, I told her to call me if something came up before she talked about it. I said, "Mother, do you want people to think you're a nut?"

She answered, "Do you mean I've dreamed all this?" I said, "Yes."

Maybe that was my mistake. From then on, she slept most of the time and refused to eat. She would not go downstairs for dinner. The nurse, Debby, reported that they sent her a tray, and she was putting the food in the garbage.

Terry, who had helped her all those years, shopping, banking and taking her to doctors' appointments, reported a change in her personality. The Director decided to put mother in "assisted living" so that aides would come in each day and take care of her. It was an extra charge, and I knew she would not accept that, so I told them not to let her know, and I paid the extra charge. When the aides came to the door, Mother kicked them out.

Debby called to tell me, "We cannot have her lying there dying.

We're sending her to the hospital for observation." I could just imagine how Mother would react being forced to go to the hospital against her will.

Terry, whom Mother loved, took her to see her doctor of forty years. He told me, "She just needs a pacemaker. Other than that, she is fine." Mother was 96, and I was concerned about anesthesia. He said, "It's a minor procedure, you do not even need to come up for it."

Henry and I were on the plane at 9:30 the next morning and there at about five. Mother was just coming out of surgery. When she awoke, she said, "Call the police. I want to have the doctor arrested. He operated on me without my permission." She went on to say, "I have a very stupid daughter to allow him to put a pacemaker in me."

I think she was right.

The healing took more of her strength, plus she had developed a bed sore which is disgraceful at a good hospital.

Before I left Florida, I had been in touch with my old friend, Josephine King, who used to work for me when I lived in Philadelphia and the children were young. Josephine had credited me with her success in life because I urged her to go to school to find a career. She was too bright to do housework. She became a doctor. She deserves a lot of credit. It was hard for African Americans in those days.

Josephine and her husband David were at the hospital when they brought Mother there from Brendenwood. Josephine said that Mother recognized her.

Josephine is a very good person and has remained a wonderful friend to me.

Mother was not "fine." She was still very feisty, but she refused to eat, even from me. She was down to seventy pounds, but the hospital was ready to discharge her.

I knew she could not go back to Brendenwood and proceeded to pack her belongings. I sent her beautiful furniture to the boys, who were happy to have it and kept what I knew she would still want for herself.

I entered her in the Royal Palm nursing home in Vero Beach. It was a beautiful place. I sent some of her clothes and belongings there so that she would have familiar surroundings. Terry arranged for movers. I gave her list of what went where.

I knew I could not manage to take both Henry and Mother on a plane. It would be more than I could handle. Josephine volunteered to take Mother to Palm Beach with David to help.

The hospital had insisted on discharging her by Tuesday, so we had to do everything fast. I left on Monday and entered Mother in Royal Palm in advance. Josephine was to bring Mother on Tuesday. When Josephine was ready to take her, the nurse in the hospital said that Mother was too weak to travel. Josephine and I decided we had to try for it.

Mother seemed to rally for the trip to Florida, and Josephine said she was excited when she heard West Palm Beach. She only complained about the bedsore which she said felt like a "rusty nail." It must have been hard for her to sit on the plane so long with that sore.

I drove to Vero Beach, and Mother sat next to me in the passenger seat, chatting all the time. She wanted very much to come to the house. "Mother," I said, "I have to get you well first." I knew if anyone could get her well, it would be this first-class facility. I guess I did not realize how bad she was. Maybe I did not want to.

When she got to the Royal Palm, she was, of course, exhausted. Josephine and David stayed at the house Tuesday and Wednesday and then went by bus to Palm Beach to see friends.

Wednesday, at the nursing home, they told me that Mother would not make it—that she was dying. They told me that it might have made a difference if she were not healing from the pacemaker surgery.

I called all my sons to tell them. Craig being with me was a big comfort. He and Kathy were with Mother as much as possible. At one point Mother reached out to touch Kyle's little hand. He went right to her side. She said, "My Kyle," and he put his hand in hers.

David left California the same day and flew all night to get there on Thursday. Mother and David had always been very close. David was in the middle of studying for his exam to become a psychotherapist, so it was not easy for him. I said to Mother on Thursday, "David is on the way." She opened her eyes and almost sat up in bed. "David is coming!" It was the last time she spoke.

When David arrived about an hour later, there was no response from her. David insisted on sleeping on the floor in her room to be near her. The nurses were fine about it. They were so kind and caring. David and I were there together, talking to Mother, hoping she could hear us. The nurse showed me how to swab her mouth with water. They no longer tried to feed her, as her body was shutting down. She had refused food there, too, although the nurses were able to get some pureed food into her with a syringe. I kept rubbing her legs and arms with body lotion. None of it seemed real. I know I was not accepting that it was happening.

On Saturday morning I was there at eight and peeped into the room. Mother was breathing quietly now, and David was asleep. I knew how tired he was. I sat outside the room to let David sleep a little longer. When I did go in, Mother was gone. David and I stayed with her before we told anyone.

She died one month shy of her ninety-seventh birthday on April 10, 1999.

I will never get the terrible image out of my memory of seeing my mother being carried off in a body bag. To this day, I will not forgive myself for not being with her when she drew her last breath.

Mother kept a diary and in it were instructions where I would find everything I needed when she died, including the cemetery plot and instructions for her funeral.

She left me the following note which was dated December 1999: "Marcy darling, I am trying to make it easy for you to take. Have David here, and Henry, if you like. Try to understand my instructions. I've changed a lot now. I am okay—no mourning. Go on with your life as if I am here. I will watch over you (if I can). Who knows!"

Henry, Craig, David and I went to New Jersey for the service. Mother's body was on the same flight. The plane trip was horrendous. United Airlines was just beginning to issue "e-tickets." When we got to the airport, they did not have tickets for us. We finally got to Atlanta, stand-by, then tried Delta, also standby. David warned the ticket agent that this was very traumatic for me, and that if I "let go," they would have a problem. I felt like I was moving in a trance, but I was on the brink of "losing it." They finally let us board the plane in Atlanta. It was a very stressful trip.

The graveside service for Mother was emotional for me, but there was closure. I left her there on a sunny windy day, with all her family around her. It was April 13, 1999. I could not help but feel "well . . . now my mother and father are together." He was buried close by in the same cemetery.

We all had lunch together, and I then left my beautiful mother amidst the spring flowers. I ordered a marker on her grave to read "We love you as high as the sky and as deep as the ocean." I will never stop missing her.

Path of Flowers by Marcy Von Kohorn

Chapter Forty-one

Response Reward Systems

I never told Mother about our financial problems with Response Reward Systems and the patents. I think she had known, as she and I had been so close. We were mother and daughter and best friends. Mother left me $350,000.

We were now living and managing fine with royalties. We also had a license with Sony for a lump sum payment. I was able to pay off Perman & Green, our patent attorneys, and the 25% for Flint.

We had gone through many legal procedures and depositions that were difficult for Henry. In many cases, I too was deposed. Henry held up beautifully, even though sometimes he could not answer questions because of his memory.

We had gone through a deposition in which Henry had a problem answering a question. The opposing attorney asked Henry if he had executed the drawings in the patent by himself. Henry answered no—the patent attorney had done the drawing according to Henry's instructions. The attorney found that if the patent attorney had not been named as a co-inventor, the patent was invalid. We did win the case, and they were forced to pay a royalty, but Flint resigned because of that deposition.

We tried many law firms after that with no success. We received a business card in the mail from John Haleak. Haleak had been the patent attorney for Catalina, and we had dealings with him when we sued Catalina. We felt he would do a good job for us and signed a contract with him in September 2001.

Haleak was to get 35% of any deals he completed. I was pinching pennies again. With Haleak in charge, we had twenty law suits going and had to support this litigation or pull out. When I tried to talk to Henry about money, he would have an anxiety attack. I was afraid he would have another stroke, so I had to carry this burden alone. I felt I was carrying the weight of the world on my shoulders. Henry had no idea of money, and it seemed impossible to limit him.

I know my health was being affected. I seemed to have a constant headache. I had dizzy spells and was not sleeping well. I was aware of strange feelings, like being pulled down into quicksand. I thought maybe this was depression. I had trouble fighting it. I felt I was caught in a trap.

We were committed and must keep on, but the financial load was wearing me down. The worst part was that there was no one I could talk to. I lost count of the number of lawyers we were paying. There was Haleak and a local attorney in Texas. Haleak found a "great" expert witness at $300 an hour. He was getting an assistant lawyer for himself at $120 an hour.

Then there were travel expenses. Craig and Haleak had to go to Texas as the judge asked for a conference between RRS and Radio Shack to see if we could come to a settlement. When Haleak traveled for us, he insisted on going first class. We were in over our heads. In three months, we spent $58,000 on lawyers. Craig was a big help to us, though now he had become a realtor. He was well suited for that profession.

We were talking to a Patent Holding Company. They would work with us on contingency, but there might be a problem with Haleak. It seems that Haleak was the worst thing that could have happened to us. He was bleeding us dry. He knew we could not afford litigation yet ensnared us into cases that would not settle.

I would have liked to have dropped all these cases, but it was not so easy. If they were dropped with prejudice, companies like Radio Shack would have the right to use the patents without paying, and word would get out that we could not defend the patents. Some of these companies had deep pockets and could afford to keep on fighting, even though they knew they were infringing.

On the positive side, we were in touch with Jamie Sigel of Sony who indicated that Sony might be interested in an exclusive license.

I now knew the patents had value and felt that sooner or later they would pay off. When we received a royalty or a paid-up license, life was good again. It was like being on a roller coaster.

In the year 2001, September 11 was the infamous day that the World Trade Center was destroyed by terrorists, and life for Americans came to a halt at this terrible attack and the loss of so many lives. Henry had been on the board of the World Trade Center, and we had been members of the famous Windows of the World, the magnificent restaurant on the top floor of the building. We celebrated the Fourth of July there, as we watched the "tall ships" come in to the harbor. It was a beautiful and a proud sight.

When something so catastrophic happened to our country, our problems seemed small in the scheme of things. We were grateful our family was safe. Our grandson Dan usually took the train into New York, the one that was destroyed, but he did not go by train that day. Bob was in New York, close enough to see the attack.

Still, life must go on. I talked to myself a lot and knew we had so many blessings. Jeff had met a lovely woman, Elizabeth, and they had a beautiful wedding on the grounds of their new house. We were getting ready to go to Connecticut for our grandson Jon's wedding. David had married Lisa who too was all we could wish for. They had a wonderful outdoor wedding in California and, shortly after, they adopted our beautiful baby granddaughter, Zoe. Kyle and Courtney are dearer to me than my own life and brought us constant joy.

Our family was growing, loving and supportive. That is a happiness that millionaires cannot buy. With all the problems I was facing, I would not trade places with anyone and, though Henry was living a fantasy, convinced we would make millions, I was glad he was alive and fully recovered from the stroke. I could never stop loving him. He was my world.

We decided it was time to sell the patents. Haleak found a man who might be interested and had great connections. Haleak went to California to meet him and also to meet with Gemstar, who showed interest. We were still dealing with cases we were trying to dismiss for lack of funds to go forward.

We then had a business reversal that was bad luck. We had sued

Landmark and received an up-front one-time payment from them of $30,000. We were receiving $56,000 per year from Cool Savings, for the life of the patent, usually 20 years. Landmark bought Cool Savings. Since Landmark had paid for a license, Cool Savings was no longer obligated to pay us a royalty. This was a huge loss and money we had counted on.

We had so far been unsuccessful in interesting anyone in buying the patents. We had depended on Haleak's help, but he was now charging us for writing letters and for UPS postage. His invoice for promotion letters came to $4800. We had an inquiry from a casino in Las Vegas. They requested a meeting, as they were interested in the gambling patents. Those were very exciting patents, and we were both thrilled to see some interest. Haleak charged us $4000 for that trip. There was no charge for the room.

I developed a rash, I think from nerves. It was all over my body and kept me awake at night. It was driving me crazy, and the doctors could not seem to help me. Finally, I was given a steroid, and that helped but made me very jumpy.

We had to raise money and to reduce our living expenses, so we decided to sell the house. I loved that house with its openness and flowing gardens, and it made me sad to leave it. Craig was doing his best to sell it. It had one flaw. The garage was in the back of the house with access to A1A. Many lookers found that a disadvantage.

We had lived there since 1987, and I had collected a lot of stuff. I started weeding out what we no longer needed. We looked at retirement homes, but our son Henry wanted us to stay in the Moorings. He was so right. We enjoyed the club, especially the tennis and had many friends here. Our son Henry even offered to put up money for us to move somewhere nice so that we would not have to wait to sell the house in order to buy. Craig took me out to look at condominiums.

I wanted to start packing but was too exhausted and had no energy. I had bouts of sweating, then water would run down my face and I would be chilled.

I did find a condo I loved. I took Henry to see it, and he too liked it. It was almost 2000 square feet, not too much smaller than our house. It was roomy with a lovely view. We put a bid on it and with a small negotiation, it was ours! I did not look back but now had a lot of work to do.

I tried again to talk myself out of depression but was boiling over in anger for Haleak. There was nothing we could do. We had a contract with him for 35%, in which he agreed to pay all out of pocket expenses. I quoted it to him as we received an email from him refusing to pay $300 for promotional letters. When I called his attention to his contract, he replied, "If you do not retract what you said by the end of the working day today, you will be very sorry."

His threats were frightening. He would send violent emails in big red letters, writing "Are you ready for Armageddon?" I never showed them to Henry.

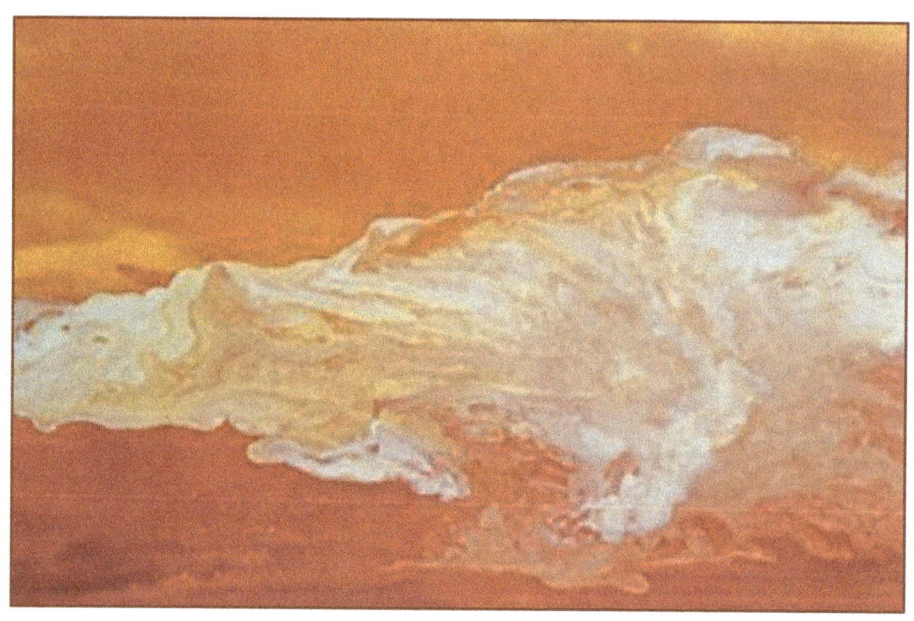

Ocean Wave by Marcy Von Kohorn

Chapter Forty-two

Moving to a Condo

W e finally sold our house to a nice young couple. I knew I would miss that house, but I also knew I had to take this next step. It helped to know we would be moving to such a lovely condominium. It seemed to be a whole new lifestyle.

We had chosen a condo on the second floor that looked out over the pool on one side and a marina on the other. I thought about Mother and how she had loved to check out who was coming and going from the second floor of her apartment at Brendenwood.

I could never imagine so many kind and caring people as were living in our building. When we went there to measure and make plans to decorate our new home, there was Bob Husbands, just coming back from the court in his tennis whites. It seemed a welcoming to this friendly community, of which we would be a part.

We were now looking at a New Year, and I asked myself why we humans think when we go to sleep on December 31 we will wake up to a bright, untroubled New Year. It was 2003, and nothing had changed. We did not spend New Year's Eve with Maggie and Glenn Johnston as we always had, as Glenn was not well. Henry and I watched the balloon come down, and then I walked down to the beach and felt one with the moon.

When I awakened on New Year's Day, I felt a sudden sharp pain down my left leg when I reached over to make the bed. It was so acute that I was unable to walk to the kitchen to make breakfast. I seemed to have no feeling from the calf down. My foot was numb. It was unbelievably painful and the beginning of six weeks of hell.

I could not sleep more than three hours (with a sleeping pill), until the spasms would wake me. I would sit in the family room all night watching television, trying to take my mind off the pain. The doctor diagnosed me as having sciatica.

When I took Henry to Dr. Scott for his Proquid injection, she asked me how I felt. When I told her my symptoms, she gave me four packets of an anti-depressant that really helped. She wrote a prayer on her prescription pad and gave it to me. She was a wonderful doctor and a wonderful person.

Henry did his best to help me. He kept asking what he could do, but he was so helpless, I was surprised he knew where the dishwasher was. At least he could put the garbage out.

Henry Jr. came to visit. When he was growing up, I could call him "little Henry," but now he had children of his own. He was no longer little, but he was a loving and caring son to us both. He went with us for Henry's appointment with Dr. Cho.

After she examined Henry, she said to me, "Marcy, hop up on the table." She took my pulse. It was 120 and she was alarmed. She gave me several tests and diagnosed me with an abnormality in the right branch of the heart. I had no idea of what that meant, but I did know that it came from stress. Dr. Cho knew it, too, as she was aware of the problems we were having with the patents and warned us both that we were destroying our health.

Once again, Henry had an encouraging conversation with the patent holding company. The company would enforce the patents, pay all expenses and after paying themselves back we would split the profits 50/50. If we accepted this deal, we would have to terminate Haleak.

We signed the contract. I was very relieved, but Haleak now claimed to own 35% of Response Reward Systems and insisted on 35% of the whole deal. He threatened to put a lien on the patents at the patent office, which would destroy the deal.

Haleak then put an assignment on the patents in the United States Trademark and Patent Office, claiming to own the patents. He transferred ownership of the patents from Response Reward Systems to Pragmatic Patent Management Company, the company owned by him and his wife, Hope Haleak. He claimed to own the patents for the "life of the patents." He also had an alias email in the name of Dr. Von Kohorn.

I called the United Stated Trademark and Patent office and asked if they had a legal department. They connected me to an attorney by the name of Mr. Roberts. I told him about Haleak, and he answered me, "Madam, if what you say is true, you are talking about conversion fraud. You will need to hire a lawyer."

There was now a cloud on the patents, and we no longer could proceed with the contract with the patent holding company. The CEO Neil suggested that we hire an attorney to deal with Haleak.

Through Neil we found an attorney named Marc Baken and decided to sue John Haleak.

Before we could gather the necessary papers for Marc, Haleak sued us. The complaint was against Henry, Marcy, Craig and General Patent. The complaint was full of inconsistences. He claimed to own the patents and later in the complaint says the patents are owned by RRS.

Marc said, "We will bury him." I did believe him, but we had to give him a $25,000 retainer. (Here we go again!) Marc was also trying to have Haleak disbarred.

Through the years, Henry had developed a professional relationship with Jamie Siegel. Jamie was interested in working with us for himself and other investors. He knew the problems we were having and, of course, could not proceed until Haleak was out of the picture.

Meanwhile, I was packing despite a torn rotator cuff and sciatica. It was not as painful as it had been, but my foot and leg were numb. My best helper was Kyle, who I picked up after school. I paid him by the difficulty of the job, and he tried to negotiate with me. I loved his "business mind."

I had Courtney putting photos in an album at one dollar per hour. She was a good little worker.

It seemed that the more I packed, the more there was to pack. I had packed sixty-six boxes so far, not counting my carefully wrapped paintings.

We had a garage sale. I practically gave things away, but we had much less space in the new condo.

Our moving date was August 13. Bob and Dana came from Connecticut to help. Craig and Kathy were there on moving day. I could not have done it without them. I made the deadline, but I will never know how.

I felt it was a new chapter in my life, a new place and a new lifestyle. I will not look back, and I will not miss the responsibility of that house. Life would be much simpler. About a month later, I had rotator cuff surgery.

Chapter Forty-three

A Deal with Jamie

Three days after rotator cuff surgery, we had a meeting with Jamie Sigel and associates Mark and Peter and Jamie's brother, Brian. They were really nice guys, and they seemed to have great respect for Henry. We met at our condominium, but I was still in bad shape from the surgery and unable to be any kind of hostess, so I ordered sandwiches from the local deli for lunch.

Basically, it was a simple deal and wonderful for us. We split everything fifty-fifty. They would handle all the legal work and pay for any litigation. We had only to collect the money and send Jamie their share.

Everything depended on breaking the contract with Haleak.

Gradually, our little condo felt like home. I would step out on my second-floor balcony at night and see the softly lighted trees, and the moon casting a shimmering path in the water. I felt like I was between heaven and earth as I looked up at the stars.

I no longer had to work in the garden in the hot summer nor replace broken sprinkler heads. Our new neighbors were kind and congenial. There were even cards to welcome us, and some angel named Gert delivered the newspaper to the door every morning.

In May we appeared in front of the judge in the courtroom in Vero Beach. John was there and requested that the "conversion complaint" against him be dismissed. (The legal term "conversion" means fraud or theft.) He also requested that his wife Hope be dismissed as a defendant. Hope was listed as president of his company Pragmatic

Patent Management, and he was employed by her. The judge denied both requests and agreed to allow the trial in sixty days. He would be the judge at our trial.

It was not until August that we were ready to go ahead with depositions. Haleak had to hire a lawyer to represent him.

On August 1, a Sunday, I picked up Marc Baken at the Palm Beach airport. I took him to the hotel and waited for him to check in. I liked him. He was decent and knew that John had been dishonest. I had prepared dinner in advance. After dinner, while Henry, Craig and Marc were talking, I had the beginning of one of my dizzy spells and retreated to the kitchen. I sat on the black kitchen chair waiting for it to pass. Craig, who always has one eye on me anyhow said, "Mom, are you all right?" I answered him, "Yes, I just need to go to the restroom." I thought if I could make it to the bedroom, I could lie down, and it would go away. When I got up, hoping I could make it, I collapsed. Fortunately, Craig was fast enough to catch me before I hit the floor.

Craig said he thought I had died. I had briefly lost consciousness. I lay down and was fine in an hour.

On August 2 we were in the Vero Beach courthouse where Marc was deposing John on the subject of using an email address in Henry's name. Marc also addressed John's almost daily email to us—in large type. "Are you ready for Armageddon?" His answer, "Oh, that was just to get Henry to come to the computer."

He lied about the letters he was supposed to write and the $300 postage, saying that the letters were really no longer effective to send at that point.

He really did not want his wife to be deposed. He had created this company when he took us on as clients. We were the only clients this company had. He claimed he was not an attorney for RRS, but that he was a consultant for PPM who employed him.

The next morning, Marc continued the deposition.

In the afternoon, Haleak's lawyer started deposing Henry. When he asked about each patent by number, Henry was able to tell him the claims of each patent. When he asked Henry why he thought Haleak had broken the contract, he focused on unimportant details, like his negative personality and his abusive language. We talked that evening.

The third day, he was questioned. Henry said that, having worked for Catalina, he could not ethically represent us and that he transferred ownership of the patents illegally. This time, he had all the facts and he was great.

John, through his attorney, made two attempts at settlements. He must have realized that he would lose at a jury trial, and maybe, in addition, would have to pay.

His first attempt had six conditions.

Marc said "I don't even want to hear your conditions. The deal is both parties walk away. The contract will no longer be in force. Or we'll go to trial."

On the second attempt, John wanted us to pay his legal expenses. It was almost lunchtime. Marc said, "We'll break for lunch. If by 1:45 we have not reached a settlement, everything is off the table, and I will depose Hope Haleak at 2 o'clock."

When we returned from lunch, John's last condition was that Craig and I swear that we had not made any money. He wanted to be paid 35% of any money that we were paid. Marc said. "Enough. Let's get on with Mrs. Haleak's deposition."

With that, John capitulated, and we had a deal, totally on our terms. What a wonderful feeling to be rid of John and his exorbitant financial demands. Now we could get on with our partnership with Jamie and his group. Now we had no more lawyers on our payroll. I felt freed!

Our settlement was in August, and as of December 1, John had still not signed the agreement. We had to go to court on December 1 to ask the judge to enforce the agreement. John's lawyer had not heard from him, and John had not returned his emails or phone calls.

The judge ordered John, through his attorney, to sign the agreement by January 7 or to appear before him, with Hope, to explain why.

There was a very good reason why the lawyer had not heard from him. Hope and John Haleak took off from the Sarasota airport in their private plane on November 4 and crashed into the ocean.

They were both dead.

The Tree of Hope by Marcy Von Kohorn

Chapter Forty-four

The Hurricanes

In September 2004, we were hit by hurricane Frances. Henry and I went to Craig and Kathy's on the mainland, as there was mandatory evacuation on the beach. It was a nightmare.

Craig had done everything possible to protect their home and to ensure our safety. When we left our condo, it was with a little prayer. I had wrapped my paintings in plastic and put them on shelves in the guest closet. (I was scheduled for another one-person show at the Elliott Museum in February.) I had not yet ordered storm shutters. In the middle of my storm preparations, there was a call from Jamie that we had a deal with Coty.

Craig and Kathy had invited a couple and their little girl to stay with us as they had to evacuate their home. The whistling and the blowing were frightening. We could not see in the dark, except with flashlights.

Kyle gave up his room for us, and Henry went to lie down. He called Craig as he thought he heard dripping water. Craig asked his father to step out while he inspected the room. The levity of the moment was that I hastened to remove the long white silk dress from the closet that I would be wearing at my art show opening. It was funny that I should think of something so frivolous at such a scary time.

Shortly after that the roof collapsed and all Kyle's possessions, including his computer, were destroyed and covered in mud. Not long after that the roof collapsed in Courtney's room where Mike and Jan were staying with their daughter. As we retreated into the family room, that roof, too, fell in. There was no let-up in the storm.

Craig and Kathy insisted on giving us their bedroom, and as we settled down for the night, the children slept on the floor in the dining room. I could not sleep and sat on a chair near them as if I could keep them safe.

I prayed a lot. In the morning there was a let-up, and we ventured outside. Trees were down and electric wires and debris were everywhere. Craig had keys to a neighbor's house across the street that Craig had agreed to watch while they were away. We were lucky to be there, with a roof over our heads, until the hurricane was over.

Craig and Kathy's house was totally destroyed, but they were able to rebuild it, although it took many months.

Back at the condo, we had no water or electricity. I was lucky to find ice at Walmart and shared it with my condo friends to keep food from spoiling.

Ten days later, we faced another hurricane named Jean, which completed the destruction of our little town. Once again, I put all my treasures in a safe place, and Henry and I drove to Orlando to escape the second storm, just as devastating.

Craig and Kathy rented a house. It too was destroyed. They moved into a condo in the Moorings that our son Henry had bought for an investment. They were not permitted to stay there as their dog Zorro weighed 10 pounds, more than the condo rules allowed. I was infuriated that people could be so small-minded at a catastrophic time like that.

Our condominium did not do well this time. We had mold and a lot of damage. Our town looked like a war zone. People had lost their roofs and all their belongings. Blue tarps covered roofs all over Vero Beach. Many people were homeless.

It took five months until our condo was repaired and livable again.

On October 25, 2004 Henry turned ninety. On his birthday, he came home from having played tennis and made himself comfortable on his favorite contour chair, which had traveled with us from the Pecksland Road days, many times being recovered. When I handed him his birthday cards, he said, with a puzzled expression on his face,

"I'm ninety today. I am going to die soon."

I told him I thought that was very funny, as he had just played tennis for one and a half hours. "Oh, sure," I said, you look like you are dying." He was even writing his own patents instead of paying a patent attorney.

It was a wonderful birthday weekend. The entire family came to celebrate him. It was a weekend that went in my *Golden Book of Memories.*

Every one of our sons and grandchildren arrived on Friday. I set up a buffet in the party room downstairs. Lisa, Zoe and David attended, although

Henry with his Sons

David was recuperating from his third shoulder operation. Emily was there and Isabelle, who had just graduated from the University of Pennsylvania Medical School. Ken's family was there, and Jeff and Elizabeth with Jon and Tara and Dan and Katie. Bob and Dana and the girls were there and, of course, Craig, Kathy and Kyle and Courtney and Faye and George.

Saturday the weather was not good, so we hung out in our condo with a lot of teasing and laughing. Little Zoe was the star and was bounced around with all her aunts and uncles. That night we had a big birthday party at the Moorings Club with one big horseshoe table and great food.

Henry, of course, was not at all excited and took it in stride. I was very grateful as I stood there and looked at our beautiful family, every one of them special in their own way.

Henry with his Grandchildren

Plum Blossoms on Gold Leaf
by Marcy Von Kohorn

Chapter Forty-five

Art Show at the Elliott Museum

Ken came from Connecticut and drove us to the Elliott Museum in Jenson Beach. The parking lot was full, and it was a thrill to think that all these people came to see my paintings.

There was a reception line. Janet Hutchinson stood at the head of the line and I stood next to her. She looked very elegant in her long gown and three-quarter white gloves. I wore the cream-colored silk chiffon palazzo pants and top that I had so carefully guarded from damage during the hurricane.

Mrs. Hutchinson was the Director and supervised the hanging. My paintings looked wonderful on the walls. Pat Patterson and his wife, Laura, did the actual hanging and were also in the reception line.

Of my family, Ken, Henry Jr. and Meredith, Craig, Kathy and the children were there. My Henry looked so handsome in his navy blazer, and I knew he was very proud of me. I felt like I was moving in a dream. I received so many compliments about my work and sold about 11 paintings.

In July we took a cruise with some of the family on the Carnival Valor. Our cabin was spacious with an outdoor balcony. I could watch the white foam of the waves at night and the path of the moon on the water. With breakfast served in the cabin and a scrumptious buffet lunch, it was easy to become spoiled. Every night the thirteen of us sat around a large table in the dining room (no salt for Henry—Lisa saw to that). There were as many courses as one could eat and delicious food. After dinner there was a fabulous show in the auditorium. It was a long walk from the cabin, so I pushed Henry in a wheel chair.

There were interesting side trips. I went off the boat once to look at the shops.

Craig, Kathy, Kyle and Courtney went snorkeling and to a monkey farm. David and Lisa and Zoe went to see the parrots, and Bob and Dana and Olivia and Melody went to a butterfly farm.

In the evening we went gambling. I won $300 on number twenty-two at roulette.

The ship was magnificent, and Henry was great. Our grandchildren had such fun together and became good friends. It was a very special week and I did not want to see it come to an end. Every time our grandchildren thanked me, I answered, "Thank YOU for making my dream come true."

Artists in Vero Beach were being asked to design and paint huge fiberglass turtles, the proceeds to benefit Mental Health. I first heard about this at a Syracuse Alumni party hosted by Ellie McCabe, who was active as a volunteer for Mental Health. She encouraged me to submit an application.

I sent in a design on paper and did not hear back, so I forgot about it. When I received a call that I was accepted and was being sponsored by the Charles Schwab Company, I thought to myself, "I must have been crazy," especially with the handicap of living in a condo and on the second floor.

I looked at every excuse I could think of to get out of doing this. I asked my friend Elaine Bush if I could paint the turtle in their garage. Elaine and Wally kindly offered the space to me and practically emptied the entire garage for my use. Even so, I had very little confidence in painting something so different.

I had never worked with acrylic paint before. I was a watercolor artist. When the enormous all-white turtle arrived, it was like the mental block I went through when I looked at a piece of rice paper before starting a new painting—only a million times worse.

That summer, I began working in the garage, with no air conditioning, but loved every minute of it. "Florida Flo" came alive to me. I worked five hours a day for a week. At the end of the five hours, Elaine rewarded me with a glass of red wine. Henry was very supportive but did not see Flo until I was finished.

The Story of Florida Flo

As I stood, feeling bare and forlorn in the garage after my long journey, somehow I knew I would become a special turtle, destined for greatness.

I was six feet tall, made of white cold fiberglass. I began to feel the warmth of a brush on my tummy. There were broad strokes of red paint forming vibrant petals of a large hibiscus flower.

I could see the artist as she stood on a ladder to give me soulful dark eyes. With each detail, I could see more clearly, and I could feel a oneness with her, as we seemed to bond and share a sense of belonging.

The softness of the brush, the carefree abandon of the artist, whose hand moved with an inner rhythm from somewhere inside the creative part of her mind. She was no more aware of the heavy August heat or of the confines of the walls or of the pots of paint scattered on her hands and clothing. She was in a different world, and I could sense a closeness as she dressed me in joyous reds, greens, and yellows, forming scattered hibiscus flowers surrounded by colorful surfboards. She thought about the design inspired by her grandson Kyle, who was a surfer.

She would take a break from time to time as her friend would bring her a glass of iced tea and comment on the transformation taking place.

Each day the paint pots would be filled, and fresh clean brushes would dance on my shell. A song filled my turtle heart, and the melody was like a duet we sang together. I sat on a base of blue water and make-believe waves that were crested by floating surf boards. A flow of Oriental energy seemed to prevail in her art as she carefully placed the vermilion lines of her Chinese seal on the corner of the base, with her signature as a finishing touch.

I was ready to go out into the world, but there was a certain sadness in our separation.

I was placed on an open truck by loving hands and carefully belted in, keeping me safe on my trip to receive a protective coating. I was left in a special place where there were other turtles. We knew we were there to preserve the beautiful designs that were painted on us.

We were then carried into a very large room where all 52 of us were gathered together. Once again, I was touched by the artist who made me such a part of her life.

Now there were many visitors to admire me and other turtles like me.

After many days on display, I was taken away from my newfound friends, as a bird is pushed out of the nest to fly on its own. I stood all by myself but was received with such joy that I felt proud. From all over Vero Beach, people would come to admire me. There were grownups and children and just tourists who had come to enjoy the ocean across from where I stood.

My artist came to see me often, and we always knew we were part of each other.

Every day there was a gentle breeze from the ocean, as I would feel the morning sun warm me. I was happy that winter brought so many visitors. Everyone wanted to have a photograph with me as they posed behind my sea-green flippers. I enjoyed the attention and hearing them say I was beautiful.

One day, at the end of winter, some men came and lifted me onto a flatbed truck. There were other turtles on the truck, all of us being removed from what had become our homes. "Oh my," one of the turtles said, "What is happening and where are we being taken?" None of us could answer as we were taken to stand under a large white tent. As much as I was happy to see my friends again, I felt lost and unhappy to be taken away from my home by the sea.

Now there was excitement in the air as we saw the tent being decorated with flowers and balloons and filled with many chairs. We learned we were to be sold at auction. It did not matter that the money would go to a good cause. "What would become of me and where would I be taken? Would I be loved? Would I be admired? Would children still come to have their pictures taken with me? Oh dear, would anyone want to buy me?" I cried, but there was no one to dry my tears. The other turtles were unhappy, too.

It was the night of the big party and auction. The guests arrived in all their finery, eating, drinking and chatting with each other, while trying to decide which one of us they would like to own.

One by one, we were displayed. The auctioneer said, "Do I hear a bid?"

We were all beautiful in our own way, but different. Some were painted with flowers, some with birds and fish. Some were bought quickly, and some had many bids and became expensive.

Then it was my turn to take the spotlight. I was nervous and frightened. A nice man kept bidding on me. A lady raised the price, but he kept going higher. Finally, the auctioneer said, "Do I hear another bid? Then—going to the gentleman in the third row." I was glad it was all over. We would be carried off again, and this would be our new home, forever. I did not know where I would be going.

There was a farewell party for us, and my artist was there and gave me a hug.

At the end of the day, one by one, we were taken to our new homes. It was then I discovered that I would stand in front of a place called Hospice House. It was a peaceful and lovely home for me, with a winding stream planted with water lilies. I stood in a place of honor near the front door.

I was not there to be admired or to be told I was beautiful. I had a far more important role to play. I was there for patients who came for comfort and care and for their friends and family. Where there were tears, I was to give them joy. Where there was sadness, I was to give them hope. I had a real purpose. I was only a fiberglass turtle, painted with a soul and given the ability to spread love and happiness. For that I am grateful to the wonderful man who bought me and placed me at Hospice House.

A Moment in Time by Marcy Von Kohorn

Chapter Forty-six

Celebrations

In January we went to San Francisco for Isabelle's wedding to Josh. I thought about the days I would tease Isabelle about changing boyfriends as often as she changed her dirty socks. She was right to wait for the real McCoy. They were perfect together.

We left from Orlando and were able to leave our car at the hotel parking lot. I knew it would be a long hard trip for Henry, but Isabelle was so dear to us that we had to try.

The wedding was held in the courtyard outdoors at the Legion of Honor Museum. It was chilly but beautiful, and Josh's father, who is a minister, conducted the ceremony. Zoe was adorable as the flower girl and my dearest Isabelle was the most beautiful bride ever.

At the wedding dinner our son Henry, Isabelle's father, brought the house down when he escorted Isabelle to the stage and sang to her, "I wish you footmen and mansions. But most of all I wish you love," and when he and Isabelle danced to a Viennese waltz, I just could not hold back the tears.

Grandpa Henry gave a speech, short and sweet, but most importantly, clean. He said he hoped that 50 years from now they would be as happy as they were now.

David was living in Menlo Park, so we went to visit him. It was a good visit except that Piccolo, the cat, got sick. It was the first time I saw their house, which David remodeled. I am always impressed with David's creativity and attention to detail.

On the trip home we again stayed at the same hotel, and when it was time for us to leave in the morning, Henry woke with such terrible gout that he was unable to put his foot on the floor to walk to the car. I had to put him in the swivel desk chair and push him from the hotel room to the car.

When I awoke on my birthday, I thought about my Mom. I talked to her and thanked her for "borning me," as I used to say when I was a little girl. I remembered, too, that she used to tell me, "It's not how you start life; it's how you end up."

I started out these eighty years with sadness, confusion and touched with meanness and hate. If it had not been for my mother, my uncles and grandparents, I could have been really unbalanced.

Like a spoiled child, I did not want to admit to my eightieth birthday, nor did I want any kind of celebration. I just wanted to skip the day altogether. Eighty is really old.

It turned out to be a wonderful day. Henry and Meredith arrived at noon, then Emily and then Ken. I received two dozen red roses from Isabelle and Josh and yellow flowers from Bob and Dana. I was showered with cards and gifts.

Craig and Kathy gave me a beautiful birthday party with balloons and flowers everywhere and a delicious dinner. It really was a celebration of love for my *Golden Book of Memories*. Everyone kept saying "You deserve it," but I don't feel that I do. I was just a mother and a grandmother and a lucky one.

So, at eighty, the woman who looks at me from the mirror is wrinkled and old, but I still feel like that young and beautiful woman who fell in love with the handsome prince and lived happily ever after. What's more, I'm still in love with the handsome prince.

April 2 was our Fiftieth wedding anniversary. There was so much to celebrate. We had an anniversary party for family and about twenty of our close friends. It was at the Quail Valley Country Club, and it was elegant. There were heartfelt speeches and a funny but wonderful one from Henry who threatened to replace me with four more wives if I did not shape up. He had me in tears. I was laughing and crying at the same time.

Chapter Forty-seven

Losing Henry

Henry was doing well for ninety-two, and at last we had no more stress from the patents. We had no maintenance fees and no attorney fees. Jamie treated Henry as a friend, with respect for his age and as an inventor. He checked in with him frequently to keep him informed. Jamie was able to interpret the claims to read that the airlines were infringing in printing boarding passes, and, in time, Southwest, United and American Airlines became licensees.

Henry slept much of the day and lay on his bed reading. He had a back problem and now walked with the help of a cane.

Henry saw a doctor at the Vero Beach Orthopedic group. The doctor diagnosed his back problem as stenosis and prescribed physical therapy, which not only did not help but his pain was getting worse. He began to lose his appetite, no matter how I tried to tempt him. He seemed to be losing his interest in living and kept telling me that we will be together "up there."

Henry believed in "life ever after" and constantly reminded me that I had better believe. When we went to church on Saturday night and said the Nicene Creed, he would poke me when we got to the part that said, "I believe in the resurrection and life ever after."

From time to time Henry had chest pains. They would come and go. Henry would see Dr. McGarry for his hemoglobin. The doctor would give him a shot of Proquid when it was too low. It was like magic and would give him back his energy

One day when we were sitting in the doctor's office, Henry had one of those attacks, and Dr McGarry ordered a chest scan. The scan showed a weakness in the wall of the aorta. Dr. Cho examined him and felt that it was not a problem, but Henry was deteriorating, and I could not help him. He could still use a walker in the condo but, by the end of the day, I would put him in a wheelchair. He tried so hard to be independent.

His hemoglobin was so low that Dr. McGarry ordered a blood transfusion, which helped, but caused his blood pressure to go up.

He developed pericarditis, an inflammation of the sac around the heart. That was why he had the chest pains and fluid in his lungs. I had given him an antibiotic when I thought he had a sore throat and that may have helped to get rid of this disease. He tried so hard and never complained but kept thanking me for helping him. His pain was only when he walked, and the doctor prescribed physical therapy.

Dr. Cho warned me to be prepared to lose him. Maybe she was right, but I would not allow fear to take over our lives.

Henry then seemed to improve. He began to eat again and seemed stronger. He still used the wheelchair, as walking was painful for him. Even getting in and out of the car was a struggle, but his hemoglobin was now perfect and there was no more fluid around his heart. We even had good financial news from Jamie.

There were still those precious days when we ended the day in each other's arms, and I knew the closeness of our love. How I wished I could put those moments in a bottle and keep them for the rest of my years. The beautiful tenderness of him, the scent of his body that was still one of strength and virility that I always loved and always will.

I would not worry but would be grateful for every day we had together. Our children came often to visit and that helped.

We went to see Dr. McGarry. He ordered a CAT scan on the pelvic area and abdomen. Dr. McGarry called me on Sunday morning to tell me that he found no problem in the pelvis and abdomen, but that he could see by that scan that the hip prosthesis was totally removed from the socket.

The orthopedic doctor never took an X-ray of the hip. That was the reason Henry had been is so much pain and, to make it worse, the doctor had ordered exercises. I should have told him to do a hip X-ray and will never forgive myself for not insisting. The pain with his hip out of the socket and trying to walk and exercise must have been unbearable.

That was a Thursday. We went right over to see Dr. Franco, our family doctor. He conferred with Dr. Cho. We all realized that Henry was a high risk for surgery but fixing his hip would take away the pain and he would be able to walk again. We went to see the surgeon and scheduled hip surgery for Monday, October 23. The doctor only had to put a new prosthesis back in the socket. The operation was a success. The doctor said the prosthesis was hanging loose in the socket. He had given Henry a spinal block, not general anesthesia, and Henry did fine.

When Henry awoke from surgery, he asked for his book—a good sign. I slept on a cot in his room Monday night. The alarm sounded on the blood pressure machine, indicating a dangerous reading. His blood pressure had plunged down at a rapid pace and stayed there. At one point it was 44/31. The nurse called Dr. Cho at home during the night.

Dr. Cho said that Henry had gone into kidney failure and was fighting for his life. She immediately changed his nephrologist to a new doctor. Henry was unresponsive, combative and seeing imaginary images. Craig and Kathy were by my side, and we bonded together, sharing love and prayers. Even through the crisis, there were snatches of his brilliance and humor. Craig tried to get him to eat something, and he kept saying, "Later." Craig said, "How much later?" Henry said, "On my ninety-fourth birthday."

He finally began to come around, and when they removed the dreaded catheter, we all took a sigh of relief. Dr. Cho said to him, "Henry, thanks for pulling through for us. You are a brilliant man and so many people love you."

Our granddaughter Isabelle, who is a doctor, told me that the kidney is so close to the hip that it got "hit" during the operation.

Gradually Henry recovered, but it took its toll. He was then transferred from the heart unit on the third to orthopedics on the fourth floor. He was there a month, and I sat in the large blue easy chair in the corner of his room from morning till night.

It was slow going and discouraging, and I have questioned my judgment 1000 times for encouraging him to go through this surgery. The night before, I asked him, "Are you sure you want to go through this operation?" He answered, "Yes." I have asked myself whether it would have been better for him to be in pain and unable to walk. At least he would have been alive. I struggled with the answer.

Lying in the hospital, he only wanted to sleep. When the therapist came, Henry would say, "Here comes the physical terrorist." He did not want visitors. The only one he enjoyed was our friend Ed Golden, who came every day, sometimes with Ann. Henry did not want to eat, although I fixed his favorite pepper soup, shrimp, stuffed eggs. Anything I could think of to tempt him.

I was despondent and discouraged, thinking that he should be better since we had brought him through the serious part. Now he was medically fine but might die because he was not eating and was not doing the therapy. He was getting weaker all the time. I was struck with the dedication of the nurses and therapists. They really tried.

I saw families clutched in the same spiral of fear as I was, and I could identify with their worried frowns. I, too, was troubled and felt helpless. Although I was told by the doctors that he was a high risk, I felt sure that it was a simple operation and that he would walk on his ninety-third birthday.

Thanksgiving Day, Craig, Kathy and the children brought the whole Thanksgiving dinner to the hospital and set up the table in the waiting room, complete with a centerpiece, turkey, stuffing, casseroles—the works. I spoke to Dr. Kane, his orthopedic doctor on the floor and asked him if he could give Henry something to allow him to enjoy this feast.

Dr. Kane gave Henry a pill called Marinol that was derived from marijuana and would give him the "munchies." He took it at 4:30, and it worked.

Kyle would go to the hospital every morning before school, get breakfast at the cafeteria and take it upstairs to eat with Grandpa. They were very close. Kyle was studying for a physics exam, and Henry was asking him questions to help him study. Henry knew every answer.

Henry and Meredith and Ken came. The family was very supportive.

I could not get Henry to do the therapy. He always had an excuse. He would not walk. After five weeks on the orthopedic floor, he was discharged to come home.

It was Dec. 2. We took his bed out of the bedroom and exchanged it for a hospital bed. As much as I was glad to have him home again, I was now a full-time caretaker. The nurse from the VNA came and also the occupational therapist. Henry refused to move, and I had to coax him to eat. I said to him in desperation, "Honey, if you do not move, you will die." He answered, "I would rather cut my life short than try to move." I had a nurse to help five hours a day, but he wanted me to do everything for him. I gave him bed baths and fed him. I wanted to do everything he asked of me. He had developed a bed sore on his heel, and we had wound care come in to treat him.

He was not improving, but we continued the occupational therapy, as we felt there was a ray of hope. Jane, the therapist, was devoted to him, and Henry liked her. We were encouraged when, with help and on his own suggestion, he got out of bed to use the potty chair.

After a while, though, even moving his legs to wash them was painful. I think the blood flow had stopped.

On December 16, Henry went on Hospice. The Hospice nurse gave me a small book to read. All the signs were there. Henry was dying. His body was just worn out, but his mind was more brilliant than ever. It was selfish to want to keep him here, but I did not know how I could live without him.

I made him his favorite pepper soup and put lots of cream in it to give him nourishment. I made him chocolate milk shakes with ice cream. I gave him Pellegrino (which he always called Gaspurilo) to keep him hydrated. He never lost his wonderful sense of humor and kept telling me, "You are doing everything just right." He loved listening to the Viennese waltzes of Johann Strauss Jr.

Bob and Dana and the girls came, and David, Lisa and Zoe. Henry kept asking for Zoe and held her little hand. Dan was here, and he and Grandpa discussed the scientific theory of entanglement.

After dinner on December 18, David suggested we do a celebration of the Advent calendar. We all gathered around Henry's bed. David hid a chocolate from Zoe in his shoe. He then made up a

Christmas story. With the glow of a candle, we made a loving, magical circle around Henry. Then Henry, his voice a little hoarse, told a story about a wise man, and I told the story about the Big Dipper. We then began to sing Christmas carols and asked Henry what he would like to sing. He answered, "Silent Night." The boys said that Dad had his sense of humor to the end, but I did not get it.

We did Advent the next night, but this time Henry did not tell a story. Again, we sang "Silent Night."

Each of his sons and grandchildren had time alone with him to say their goodbyes. They had all been with him these weeks.

On Friday the twenty-second of December there was a sudden deterioration, and I became very frightened. Henry began breathing like a fish out of water and could no longer speak, except with his eyes which seemed so troubled. He appeared frightened and was struggling.

I sat with him all day, talking to him. I knew he could hear me as I knew the hearing was the last thing to go. I told him that it was okay to go and that he was going to a better place—that his job was done here. I talked to him about our wonderful family and told him that I would be all right. I told him how much I loved him and that our love would reach beyond the stars, that it was as big as the universe. I asked him if he could leave me pennies to let me know he was with me. Barely audible now, he told me he loved me. It was terrible to watch his struggle with death.

At 10 o'clock on Saturday night, December 23, I went to bed. I was so very tired. I said to him, "Darling, I am going to sleep now. I will be here right next to you, where I belong." I fell asleep but woke often. When I awoke at 1:15, he was gone.

Without his soul, it no longer looked like Henry. There was a tear on his cheek. I first called out to him but then sat there, crying, holding him in my arms, quietly talking to him before I went to wake David and Lisa. I was so grateful they were there. Lisa's own mother was dying, and yet they stayed on to be with me.

Craig and Kathy were there in fifteen minutes, and Craig called Hospice as he was instructed. A lovely nurse named Tiffany came and tenderly washed him in a beautiful and ritualistic way to prepare his body, at the same time comforting me. It was December 24.

Our son Henry wrote a beautiful obituary that appeared in the *Vero Beach Press Journal, The Greenwich Times,* and *The New York Times.* Jeff called all our good friends to tell them.

Three days later, we had a church service at Our Savior Lutheran Church. When I saw him now, in the casket, he looked peaceful, and I thought he had a little smile on his face. The church was crowded with family and friends. Our son Henry sat next to me and was a great comfort to me.

Henry, Ken and Jeff spoke and were eloquent. I asked Eric to sing and, although he was not prepared, he sang a piece called "Eclipse." His voice was vibrant and beautiful.

A strange thing happened the morning of the funeral. My friend, Cheryl, who lives in the condo next door, told me, with tears in her eyes, that the night before at about 2 a.m., she and her husband Gene were both awakened by a noise. She told me that Gene looked out the sliding doors, and she opened the front door to look at the hallway. She saw Henry walking through my front door. Cheryl and Gene are down-to-earth people and not subject to dramatics. Their story somehow got me through the day.

On December 29, we gathered at our family plot at the Putnam Cemetery in Greenwich, Connecticut. It was a raw day, and Meredith wrapped me in her brown Persian lamb coat. Henry always told me I was beautiful, and I tried to be for him, though my heart was broken. Ken conducted a meaningful and beautiful graveside service. Eric sang magnificently. I knew he did that for me. Many of our dear friends were there. It was hard, so very hard, when they lowered the casket. I could not bear knowing I would never see him again, until we meet again in Heaven.

We went back to Henry and Meredith's for a reception. It was a perfectly arranged table with delicious food. Everything was a blur. I don't know how I was able to speak to anyone, but I appreciated that they were there, especially our partner Jamie Siegel and his wife.

The next day, our family met at Jeff and Elizabeth's, and with the warmth of a fire in the fireplace and a fabulous buffet dinner in their cozy kitchen, I found comfort in the love of family.

Iris by Marcy Von Kohorn

Chapter Forty-eight

Leave Me a Penny

I felt that it was the end of my journey, and perhaps I should end my story here as well. I walked around in something of a daze. I found it strange that the world would go on. It should be like the sleeping castle where everything stopped.

Each night I stood on my little balcony and looked up at the stars. The moon seemed bright but so far away; I kept wondering where Henry was and asking him to come to me in my dreams. I felt his presence in the gentle breeze and imagined he was near me.

I tried to hide from people. If I went to the market, I would avoid having to say hello to anyone I knew. I had no zest for living and no interest.

Craig and Kathy were wonderful. Craig told me that we were receiving a huge sum from Southwest Airlines. I wished Henry could have lived to see his patents successful. I used to think, "If I had that kind of money, I could do so many fun things," but now I did not care.

I talked to Henry when I took my walk, and I wrote to him. I began to find pennies. I found some downstairs in the lobby and at the back door and some just at different places. I knew he was with me.

My darling, I shall never forget how blue your eyes were.

I shall never forget the sound of your voice when you called "Maaarcy."

I shall never forget the faraway look in your eyes when we played the Strauss music at dinner time.

I shall never forget your touch. When you held me in your arms, I wanted to stay there forever.

I shall never forget the scent of you that only a woman knows of her man.

I shall never forget the small tear on your cheek when you were dying. And the smile on your face when I saw you for the last time.

I shall never forget the raw abandon with which I loved you when we met and until you died.

Now and forever, I can't get over losing you, no matter what I do. I'm all tangled up inside.

Somehow it seemed important to me that I see Ralph and Jill in New Zealand. I don't know what I expected, but maybe I would find a part of Henry in his brother Ralph. I announced to Craig and Kathy that I was going to see Ralph and Jill who were now in their vacation flat in Maroochydore, Australia. Craig and Kathy and Kyle and Courtney insisted on going with me.

There is a fascinating story about the title bestowed on Henry's father Oscar because of his invention of Rayon. Ralph and Jill enjoyed using the title on calling cards, and the crest was embroidered on their clothing. The title is hereditary. The crest goes back to a Dutch Cohern family from 1630, with a coat of arms of a cow horn to which Oscar added a joker. Valerie added the additional "zu" (*from* in German) and invented a mythical city to be "*zu Korning.*" This all took place before the Communist Socialist Revolution.

I have no idea how much Henry knew or how much he did not choose to remember. The strange thing is that Henry left so much of the past in his file cabinets for me to find, German documents, naturalization papers, old passports, and many photos of their palatial home. I found all this when I started searching for material for an obituary.

I had last minute doubts about taking this trip, but if I stayed in Vero Beach that summer, I would continue to feel alone, isolated and depressed. Part of me did not want to leave this little condominium as I felt that Henry was here in every corner. I did not want to leave him, but I knew that was not realistic. I am alone. He is gone, and there is nothing left of him except the chair he sat in, his Johann Strauss CDs, and my memories. I knew if I left it would help me from hurting so much, and when I returned, I might be able to accept my life as it would be without Henry.

Chapter Forty-nine

Chemnitz, Germany

It was June when we left from Ft Lauderdale and arrived in Frankfort, Germany. We traveled by train to Chemnitz. The conductor was a little man with thick glasses and a red cap, right out of an old movie. I felt like I was also living in that movie, as a little old woman, traveling with my family, living out an unknown destiny.

In Germany we learned of events that took place when Oscar and Valerie were married. We learned about their lives, their achievements and the world they left behind in Germany when it became infested with the Nazis who built a killing machine that was able to take over the minds of a whole nation. As I watched the gentle green landscape through the window of the train, I could glimpse the people who lived through the horrors of those years. I mourn for those who now seemed so real to me. As the train chugged along, stopping at each quaint station along the way, we finally arrived at our destination, Chemnitz, where Henry was born. It was not at all the station of a sleepy little village.

Once again, Craig, and Kyle passed our suitcases from the train to the platform and then piled them onto two luggage carts which they pushed up the hill to the hotel. When we finally reached the Chemnitzer Hotel, Ken and Jeff, followed by their wives, rushed off the terrace to meet us. I felt none of this was real, the antiquity of the buildings, the chiming of the bells from the church tower, and our family together to share this wonderful experience.

The next day we arrived at 35 Parkstrasse and had a tour of the house where my Henry had grown up. Lars, who bought the house, was restoring it. He showed us the many rooms and details already returned to their original form. As we climbed the steps to see the bedrooms, I could visualize the large canopied bed in the photos I found in Henry's office after he died.

We found the music room, which Henry had talked about, where famous composers like Richard Strauss joined in musicales with Henry's mother and other famous musicians. We found Henry and Ralph's playroom and their bedrooms.

I could feel Henry there.

The back stairs were still the original steps and very steep as we climbed to the very top of the tower where we could see the entire city. We walked around the grounds and saw the park where the pool and tennis courts had been. A little further was the caretaker's cottage. It was a large and impressive villa.

The next day, we went to Durmoul to see where Vati was born. Durmoul is part of Bohemia, now in the Czech Republic. Lars drove us in his large van. It was a long ride from Chemnitz, but the countryside was beautiful. We also walked around an old cemetery searching for ancestors. We found a large tombstone for Marcus Alexander Kohorn, Vati's grandfather. He would have been Henry's great grandfather.

On our way out of town, we went to see the Metropol Theater, which Vati had purchased for Mutti to give large and elaborate dinner parties. We did not go inside.

A few days later, Ken and Jeff and their wives left for Prague. We had such a good time with them. Our family does have a wonderful togetherness. We had so much fun and real belly laughs. I was teary eyed when they left.

When we left Chemnitz for Munich, we stopped at an old town called Regensburg. We walked on the narrow ancient streets and passed a beautiful old church and a holy house built by a famous Israeli architect.

Chapter Fifty

The Eiffel Tower

From Munich, we took the train to Stuttgart and from there to Paris, arriving at twilight. The boulevard along the Seine on the way to the hotel was just as I remembered, with fountains, lights, statues and upscale department stores that brought back many memories. The lights twinkled on the Eiffel Tower as if to welcome us.

Craig bought walkie-talkies (no cell phones yet). It was a brilliant idea as we needed two taxis with all our luggage.

We pulled up to the Ramada Hotel. It was not the fashionable hotel I was used to. Henry had always spoiled me. My room was on the top floor facing the overhead trains and surrounded by typical French apartment buildings.

It was about 11 at night when we arrived. I was ready for bed, but Craig, Kathy, Kyle and Courtney walked to see the Eiffel Tower.

The next day the five of us went sightseeing. Kyle had studied the subway system and got us to the Louvre, where we passed through a courtyard to a large glass pyramid and into the huge lobby of the Museum. As we approached the long steep escalator, we watched in horror as a woman tripped on one of the steps and tumbled down the escalator, bouncing like a rag doll. The escalator stopped, and with all the medical personnel and excitement, we left without seeing the exhibits.

We walked out into a heavy rain, bought a few umbrellas, and found a nice café where we could eat, dry out and regroup. Tired, wet and discouraged at a wasted day in Paris, we then stood in line for a taxi back to the hotel.

That evening it stopped raining and, after a rest, we walked leisurely to the Eiffel Tower, stopping here and there to see the shops.

The Eiffel Tower was awesome. Craig bought tickets for us to go to the top, with loud "NOs" from Kathy and me, but up we went. Standing in line, we met tourists from Orlando, Tampa and Melbourne, Florida. At the first landing we walked around the circular platform, looking at the wondrous sights of Paris. It was about eight in the evening when we arrived, and though it was still light, it was cloudy. We then walked up a flight of steps to the elevator that took us to the summit. From there, Paris looked like a toy city. Like magic, the sky began to clear, and radiant rays of sun turned Paris into specks of gold. The sky was ethereal and looked like pictures of Heaven. Maybe it was Paradise. I wondered if I would always be thinking in this crazy way, seeking Henry everywhere.

Walking back, as we looked at the majesty of the Eiffel Tower, it now blinked with bursts of sparkling, flashing lights. It was an exciting and wondrous sight.

Hungry now and with the dark clouds leaving the sky with the pink remains of the sun, we found a café where we had dinner. We choked when we received the check. Even a coke was eight dollars. No matter. It was Paris, and we had a lovely evening.

The next day, we took a very elegant van with an equally elegant driver, to the railroad station to board the Chunnel train to England. On the way, the driver gave us a fast tour, driving by many important landmarks, including a drive under the Arch de Triumph. Paris is beautiful.

I was not aware of anything special about the famous train we boarded, except that it connected Paris to London through a tunnel under the Channel, hence the name Chunnel.

At the railway station in London, we found a woman working at the information desk who was very helpful. She arranged for a large van at a good price to take us to our hotel at the airport, which Craig had booked. My single room was right across from Kyle and Courtney's. It was such a joy for me to be greeted by them in the morning and to get a kiss goodnight.

We had tickets for the theater and cleaned up pretty well. The Palace Theater was old and interesting. When we took our seats, my young handsome grandson wanted to go to the bar to get something to drink. We went together, and he asked for a split of champagne. The bartender hesitated because of Kyle's age, so I told him it was okay. I would pay for it.

Back at the seat, Kyle poured the champagne and shared it with Kathy and me.

The show was hilariously funny and so well done. It was Monty Python. Henry would have loved it.

The next day we again went sightseeing and again Kyle figured out public transportation for us to get to London from our hotel in Heathrow. We found an open tour bus—we got off at the Parliament and took pictures in front of Big Ben. We saw Westminster Abbey and explored St. Margaret's Cathedral with all its ancient and interesting crypts. We walked around the "Eye," the famous Ferris wheel, and along the Thames River.

Back on the bus, we were intrigued when the tour guide pointed out a lingerie shop where "the Queen buys her underwear." We passed on that, but when Craig spotted the Rolls Royce showroom, he hustled us off the bus. He wanted so much to find Vati's old Rolls Royce that had been ordered in London and fitted out in Paris.

We walked into the Rolls Royce dealership, none of us intimidated by the plush surroundings and personnel. Craig explained the circumstances, adding that he knew the company kept records of purchases, but it seemed that their records did not go that far back.

Meanwhile, Kyle was sitting behind the wheel of a pretty spiffy car and Kathy in a convertible in which she looked as though she belonged. I discovered the ladies room that was so luxurious we girls had to "freshen up."

We checked out the store where the Queen buys her underwear, and I thought, if that's the kind of underwear the Queen wears, I shall have to have a serious talk with her.

After a quick lunch, we went to see the changing of the guard at Buckingham Palace. The guards really did look like statues.

The last part of our tour took us to the old part of London where the great fire had started. The tour guide also told us about the plague.

It was dinnertime. We were bedraggled and hungry, plus which we had to duck the raindrops. We were in Piccadilly, and Craig wanted to find somewhere adventuresome to eat our dinner. Kathy wanted fish and chips. We ended up in the theater district in a steakhouse which did not please anyone, but it was food. We took the underground back to our hotel on the route planned by our expert navigator.

I cherished my goodnight kiss from Kyle and Courtney!

Chapter Fifty-one

Down Under

The family insisted that I take this long trip from England to Australia in business class. I felt guilty leaving them in the coach section and enjoying this luxury. Paul, the attendant, hovered over me, mindful of my every wish. My gourmet dinner was delicious and served with a lovely wine.

Paul showed me how to turn my seat into a bed, gave me cozy pajamas, and even tucked me in with a soft blanket. I slept well.

Breakfast was even more gourmet with scrambled eggs, nova salmon, a croissant and coffee.

We disembarked at Singapore, where I helped Kyle choose a perfume for his girlfriend. Then back on board for our final leg to Sydney.

We checked into the hotel in Sydney and went to see my sister-in-law Dee the next evening. When Dee and Ralph were living in White Plains, Dee was my dearest friend. That was a long time ago. I had never met her new husband John whom she married when she moved back to Australia with the children. I wondered if we would still feel this special friendship or if it would be a formal stilted evening. The only time I ever heard from Dee was at Christmas when we exchanged cards.

Arriving at the door, I saw that the house was impressive and right on Sydney Bay. Inside, we were greeted warmly. Dee and I hugged each other like long lost sisters. What memories flashed through my mind. In my eyes she looked the same. Next year to be eighty, but I had a feeling she might be having health issues. She looked frail.

It was good to see Steven. He and Craig seemed to bond right away. Steve's wife Annette was more beautiful than ever. I felt sadness for the break between Steve and Ralph. How foolish to continue the hatred between father and son. What precious time is lost, and probably for Ralph's lifetime.

I guess I cannot walk in someone else's shoes.

Steve has spent a great deal on patents, and he and Annette were sure they would be very rich one day. I knew all about that—I had walked that walk.

Jacquie is gorgeous. She is studying law. Marcus Alexander is in a private school in advanced classes and "head boy." I wondered at the coincidence, having seen the tombstone in Germany of his great grandfather, also named Marcus Alexander. Piers was also in a private school and very bright. He was the youngest of Dee's grandchildren. Their mother Karen was charming and attractive as always.

I visited with each one and felt a warm relationship with each, but mostly with Dee. Her husband John was not well enough to join us.

Craig, Kathy, Kyle & Courtney in Sydney, Australia

The buffet dinner was sumptuous. The table looked like something from a magazine. Drinks and hors d'oeuvres were served by the butler, Joe. They even had a birthday cake for me.

We stayed until 11:30 and left reluctantly. I did feel a kinship with this little family and was very emotional about my reunion with Dee.

We left the next day for our flight to Brisbane. Ralph and Jill were at the gate to meet us.

The apartment in Maroochdyre was amazing. It was large and comfortable and faced the ocean. What a magnificent welcome they gave us.

On the front door was a sign that read "Villa Kohorn." On my door was a sign "Froufrou Kohorn." Each sign was professionally done and laminated.

Jill rented the vacant apartment next door for Craig, Kathy, Kyle and Courtney. There were gorgeous flowers everywhere and beautiful yellow ones in my room. Jill had even arranged for Kyle to have a surf board and a wet-suit and all the equipment he needed.

The Siamese cat Minky is their pride and joy, but I hurt when Ralph referred to the cat as his son.

Jill was just as beautiful as ever with her blonde hair always handsomely coiffed. She is a marvelous cook and had planned and prepared unbelievably delicious meals for us. When the weather was nice, we ate on the outdoor porch upstairs, with torches lit so dramatic when the sun went down.

I was overwhelmed with her creativity, attention to every detail and warm generosity. She even arranged for a massage for me every day. She treated me like a princess. I felt so close to Jill but found nothing of Henry in Ralph, which I had come here looking for.

Kyle was out surfing every morning. Sometimes we watched him from across the street, and other times I sat on the beach watching him.

He was in heaven, and the waves were great.

Jill arranged for something special for the family every day. They went to the zoo. They went bungee jumping. They went to drive the racing cars, and Kyle went scuba diving with sharks.

Ralph had his trainer named Cathy. He did very well under the circumstances but used a cane, a walker and sometimes needed a wheelchair. Jill kept him as healthy as possible and was devoted to him.

Every once in a while, when Jill became totally exhausted, she would have him entered into a nursing home for respite. They would make him feel like a VIP and catered to his every whim. He seemed to enjoy going there, but knowing Ralph, he may just have said so to make Jill feel good about it.

The family went home, but I stayed on. Jill would put me out on the terrace with a book and a glass of red wine while she made dinner. She was very sensitive to my state of mourning.

I stayed with Ralph and Jill for a month and loved every minute of it. Often Jill and I went very early to the outdoor market, and I bought a few things for the cool weather there.

We had a visit from Jill's niece Cheryl, whom I really connected with, and her adorable little daughter Katlin. They were going to New Zealand, and I took the opportunity to travel with them to see my very dear friend Dick Potton in Nelson. He was living with Elspeth. She and I became friends, and they made me feel so welcome. Dick took us to the movies. (He owned the movie house.) We had a private showing in a small dining room where we were served lunch.

Elspeth took me for a ride after the movie and showed me the hospital that Dick had founded and still maintains. He also started Hospice House there.

Dick's home was exquisite, and every detail was perfection. He had always been special to me, and I was distressed to see that he was not in good health. He was painfully thin and seemed even more deformed from the polio. He was stooped, and his head hung forward as if it was barely connected to his body. I was there from Thursday to Saturday, and Dick died the following Saturday. Elspeth told us that he had fallen in the shower and had broken his arm. He was in the hospital, alert and talking to her, and the next minute he was gone. I was so glad that I had taken this trip to see him.

As I walked through the airport to return to Brisbane and Maroochydre, I passed a small enclosed atrium with a huge rock behind the glass and a coin sitting on the rock. I was still looking for the pennies I had asked Henry to leave me. I never stopped thinking of him.

Once back with Ralph and Jill, I began sorting out what I would take to China with me and mailed back two boxes of excess clothing. I was nervous about going to China alone and worried that maybe the tour guide would not meet me.

Marcy in China

Chapter Fifty-two

China

Again in business class and treated royally on Qantas Airlines, I arrived in Beijing at 8:10 p.m. local time. I was relieved when I saw my tour guide holding a sign with my name on it. I waited while he greeted another member of our group, an Australian, and we were taken by van to the hotel. The hotel was first rate and the room, too. By the time I got settled in, it was midnight, two in the morning Australian time, and I was tired.

My tour buddy, who arrived on the same flight, called to check in, and we met in the lobby for breakfast and then for lunch. His name was Jim Ryan. We walked to a restaurant and, as the menu was all in Chinese, we pointed to what we wanted. Afterward, we walked to a supermarket for a few items such as water and milk. I helped Jim figure out the code for the safe in his room. It was nice to have a friend. Jim was married but traveled a great deal without his wife. That night we had dinner and then went for an after-dinner drink on the 26th floor, where we could look down on the lights of Beijing.

The tour began officially the next day, which was a Sunday. We had a new tour director named Lee. The group met at eight, and we went to Tiananmen Square, which was huge and crowded with people of all nationalities and all walks of life. There was a museum of antiquities and the mausoleum where Chairman Mao is preserved lying in a crystal coffin. There was the Great Hall of the People and many vendors selling toys, post cards, kites and everything imaginable.

It is a strange feeling for me to be conscious of my age as I only became an old lady when Henry died, so it was new for me to have people treat me as old. The Chinese show great respect for their elders. I never did feel old, but when I look in the mirror, I do see a wrinkled face, and I wonder how this old lady got into my mirror.

We then went to the Forbidden City, where the emperors lived from 1400 to 1911. It was most impressive and over 240 acres. We walked from large courtyards up hundreds of steps into many palaces, peeping into bedrooms, throne rooms and all kinds of halls with lovely antique furnishings.

With so many tourists, I had to keep my eye on the blue flag our leader carried, so not to get lost. I was jammed in between crowds of humanity, and I was conscious of how easy it would be to be shoved or to lose my balance with all the bodies pushing each and every way. I was grateful that Jim was close behind me in case I did not manage the steep steps. I finally was on top and able to look down at the courtyard from the palaces. There were hundreds of guides with tours following their flags up and down stone steps and through narrow passageways, weaving in and out of courtyards.

After a wonderful lunch we went to the Summer Palace, again with lots of walking.

At the start of the Sacred Way, there was a large lotus garden on a lake with pale pink and white blossoms and enormous flat lotus leaves. I walked around the lotus pond, feeling very emotional, as

Lotus by Marcy Von Kohorn

the lotus has always been so special in my study of Chinese painting. The lotus is very sacred to many religions and signifies the cycle of life. The flower opens and closes three times. On the third day, the petals are carried by the wind and the pod hangs down, allowing the seeds to fall into the mud, from which another flower grows.

I then noticed a large green leaf with a coin in the center and thought maybe Henry was letting me know he was with me. As my mother would say, "Who knows?"

I made friends with an Australian couple, Monty and Mike, and also developed a friendship with Jim. He said, "What would my wife say if she knew I was with an American lady?" I answered, "She would probably be happy you had company." He talked a lot about his family and his new grandchild.

Monty and Mike were from Adelaide. Monty had white hair and a pink English complexion. Mike was tall, slender and very energetic. He was a well-known scientist and worked on laser mapping. He and Henry would have liked each other.

We went on a long covered walkway with small paintings on the overhang ceiling and benches to rest. The "serenity" walk went on and on and seemed endless until we came to the "marble boat," built to look like marble and built on a platform. It almost looked real. We then boarded a sightseeing boat for a ride around the huge man-made lake. After dinner there was a show, but I had had enough for one day.

The next day, we had an early start and went to the Ming Tomb. Walking along the road to the tomb, I saw some elder gentlemen who had a huge brush, the size of a broom. They dipped the brush into water and wrote calligraphy characters on the cement pavement. I stopped and so did my group. I asked by "pantomime" to have the brush. I then dipped the brush into the water and wrote the calligraphy for love (which is my favorite). At first, the men looked like I was an "ugly American," but then looked at me with admiration, as though we were friends. My tour group said I was their "star." At the Ming Tomb there again were steep steps and many ancient sites.

There was also a covered pit where the concubines were buried when the emperor died. They were dropped into the pit, feet first, alive.

From there we drove to the famous Great Wall surrounded by

magnificent mountains. It was thrilling to see.

At the base we could decide how far up we wanted to climb. Jim and I chose the short climb which was steep enough. I had to extend my body forward to walk. I was grateful that I had someone to look out for me, as it was difficult climbing and there were steps as far as the eye could see. We held onto the handrail and watched young and old and many different nationalities hiking their way up. You could see the steps and interim platforms for miles (the brochure said 3600 miles) and when we looked down it almost made me dizzy. On the way down, I found myself leaning backward to walk and when we got close to the bottom, we stopped at a small café for a cold beer.

At dinner there was a show of four boring skits in Chinese, so it was a late night, and I got to bed close to midnight.

The next morning, as we climbed to the Temple of Heaven, I watched in amazement as everywhere there were people doing Tai Chi and ballroom dancing to music, playing with racquets and balls and exercising.

The path was lined with stone animals, one side standing as though on duty and on the other side standing as though off duty. As we approached the exit, we were ushered into a pedicab, which has a seat big enough for two, with a man on a bicycle towing our little carriage behind him.

We went through narrow alleys, passing homes and looking at families and their lifestyle. I felt that if I were living in one of those houses, I would resent the foreigners intruding this way.

We then stopped at one of these houses and were shown into a courtyard. The daughter-in-law showed us the rooms in this house and how they lived. Their home was very, very old but kept in good condition. It was taken away from the family during the Cultural Revolution but afterward returned to the family.

The old mother and father had the senior rooms. They were shown great honor and were resting. We saw the other bedrooms, the extensive kitchen and dining room, and also an art studio for the husband and brother who cut out folk art. The overhead latticework ceiling in the courtyard was hung with grapes, tomatoes, pumpkins and other kinds of fruit and vegetables open to the sun. The house had several televisions and computers.

Dinner was an absolutely delicious Peking duck. I begged off the evening entertainment. I knew the group was meeting at 5:30 the next morning to go to Xian.

We had an 8:30 flight and were met by a new guide named Vincent. The group then split up, as some were going on a riverboat. Jim took the river tour, but I was glad Monty and Mike were still with me. We were taken to a museum of history and to a pagoda to see a Buddhist temple with lovely gardens and finally to check in at the hotel at four.

The following morning as I was going downstairs to meet with my tour group, I had one of my attacks. I sat in the bus, hoping it would pass. My heart was pounding, I had a fast pulse, and I was in a cold sweat. I looked for Monty to help me. She was a nurse. She and the guide, Vincent, helped me to walk to a wooden bench. I felt close to fainting. I was aware that people stopped to wonder why this old lady was lying on the bench, but it all seemed far away to me. The guide came by several times to check on me, and Monty took my pulse. It was racing at 120. Finally, after what seemed to be a long time, it subsided, and I felt well enough to continue the tour.

Monty later wrote a medical note for me to take to the doctor. She and Mike stayed close to me as we continued on to see the terra cotta warriors, which were incredible, with faces exactly like the original warriors. Even the horses were amazing. Not one of them looked alike. I had read about this discovery some time ago. A farmer was digging in his field and came across this huge underground army, each one totally different.

Dinner was dim sum, all kinds of wonderful dumplings and a fabulous show.

We met in the morning at 8:00 to make a flight to Shanghai. I called Craig using a telephone card, as I had not been in touch, and it occurred to me that they might be worried about me. They were!

The group was again split up, and some of them went to Guilan. In Shanghai, our guide took us shopping on the famous Nanking Road and to see more gardens. After lunch we went on a boat ride on the river—very relaxing. That night after dinner we were treated to a great acrobatic show.

The next day we finally got to the Shanghai Art Museum. That was so special for me. I went off on my own and spent all my time looking at old paintings and calligraphy.

We walked to a restaurant and had an easy, warm, compatible dinner with our group. We had now become good friends. It would be our last evening together, so after dinner, we sat in the lobby and shared a bottle of wine.

Jim and I had breakfast in the morning. I was quite concerned as he seemed to have developed a bad cold and looked feverish. Monty and Mike joined us, and there were sad farewells to all.

The driver dropped me off at the airport, and now I was really on my own. My travel agent had booked me on a flight to San Francisco so I could visit David and Lisa on the way home.

The plane to Beijing was delayed because of bad weather, and I hoped I would not miss my connection. The plane circled the airport, trying to land, but then the pilot announced that because of weather conditions we would land in Delian to wait till it cleared. I was now flying Air China. Delian is on the coast and is about a two-hour flight from Korea.

We sat on the plane for ten hours. There were many angry, frustrated passengers. I was glad I was sitting in business class and at least was comfortable. A young American man sat across from me. He was very kind and allowed me to use his cell phone to call Craig. People were shouting and asking questions of the crew, with no answers. Someone had called Beijing and was told it was only a light rain.

The crew ran out of food and water, and passengers were shouting, "We are being held prisoners; let us off the plane!"

They finally brought a bus to the plane, took off our luggage and instructed us to disembark. We were taken by bus to a shabby old hotel in the city of Delian. We carried our suitcases into a threadbare lobby and lined up for room assignments. I was paired up with a young Chinese woman. Despite the circumstances, being old has its advantages in Chinese culture, as I was treated with great respect and courtesy because of my age. A nice couple even carried my bags up the steps to my room, as there was no elevator.

We were told we would get a wake-up call in the morning, at which time we would meet in the lobby and would receive more information.

The room had twin beds and was about as meager and spare as it could be. The carpet was torn and stained, and the paint was peeling off the walls. Even my roommate said, "This is bad."

I spent a pretty miserable night, although I did get a shower and brushed my teeth with water from the faucet—fingers crossed. At six o'clock, we received a phone call to meet downstairs for breakfast at seven. We walked down the street in this primitive, backward town to a restaurant. We sat at round tables and were served Chinese gruel, some kind of meat, rice, raw dough buns and other unrecognizable food. I picked at something that might have been a greasy overcooked fried egg. I asked for tea, which helped.

We walked back to the hotel and were taken by bus to the Delian airport where we were separated into two groups; I was in the one to Beijing and San Francisco. There were about seventy-three people going to San Francisco, so I was hopeful the airline would make some arrangements for us. No one had any idea of what was happening.

After going through customs and a two-hour wait in the airport, we took off in such a heavy fog that you could barely see the wings. The stewardess told me that the Delian airport was closed after we took off.

On arrival, we followed the attendant with a sign for SFO passengers, through crowds to collect our luggage and then were led to the next floor, where there were many lines of people to reschedule flights. It was now about three. My flight was to leave at four. I had had nothing to eat or drink since breakfast.

I went to the business class window, pushing a cart with my luggage. Wrong window. I was sent to another. At the next window, I was told that the four o'clock flight was full. Again, I was sent to another window, and there was told to come back tomorrow morning. I then went to another window, and this time I pretended to be ill, close to fainting and asked for help. I was told to see the manager who told me to try United. I went to United and, oh, how good it was to communicate in English! The agent said there was a flight leaving in fifteen minutes for Washington D.C. with one seat available. Did I want it? I would have gone anywhere to get to the U.S. and away from this madhouse. It was now 5:30 and, without food all day, I was feeling weak and weary.

I absorbed the sounds and sights of the USA on an American carrier and was glad to speak English and to be understood,

I found my window seat on the upper deck next to a nice man from the State Department. I crashed into the comfortable seat and blessed Henry for insisting that I travel business class. I borrowed a cell phone and called Craig to let him and the family know I was safe and on my way home.

After a wonderful steak dinner and three glasses of red wine, I fell into a deep sleep of exhaustion. We were awakened two hours before landing. I went back to the kitchen after our morning snack and spoke to the stewardess. I told her my harrowing story and asked her if she could help me reschedule my flight to Florida. I was fresh out of energy and knew I could not deal with going from Washington to San Francisco. She said she would radio ahead and have a United ground crew person help me.

When we landed and went through customs and while at the carousel getting my luggage, the same stewardess came over to me and pointed out a desk behind me where there were two United attendants. They helped me reschedule my flight to Orlando, Florida. I decided to get a night's sleep rather than getting to Orlando at midnight. The United manager got me a room at the Hyatt. It was now 9:30 pm.

I took the shuttle bus to the hotel where I had a sandwich and a glass of milk and called Craig to meet me and to tell David to cancel my visit. I found my room and went to sleep. Once back in Florida, I was so glad to see Craig at the airport. It was not a good ending, but nothing could spoil my trip to China.

Chapter Fifty-three

Connecticut

It was so good to be with my family again. I had a welcome home party at Craig and Kathy's. In October I was able to visit David, Lisa and Zoe in Menlo Park.

When I went to Connecticut in the fall, Jeff took me to see Isabelle just out of the hospital with my new great grandson, Emerson. Our family was growing so quickly; I think we were becoming a dynasty! It was a good visit to see family and friends. I had dinner with Toni and Ralph Wyman, met with Karen Sadik Khan and had lunch with the Phillips. Estelle is now gone.

I spent a quiet time visiting Henry at the cemetery under the lovely Japanese maple tree.

I also spent a few days with Bob and Dana and the girls.

Shortly after, there was a baby shower for Katie, Dan's wife. It was obvious that Katie was very uncomfortable. As it happened, she really was in labor, and after a wild drive to the hospital, Ella was born.

I had a date with my step sister, Susie, with whom I had reconciled. I never thought it would be possible for me to forgive her, but forgiveness is so good for the soul. Even though for years I suffered with anger for what she and Jackie had done, it was good to let go of that anger.

We were still having the same legal problems with the patents, even though we now had such decent and honest lawyers. Jamie had brought on the firm of Kenyon and Kenyon. They sent a car for me to go to their offices to familiarize me with the kind of questions I would be asked in a deposition.

The office was at the tip of Manhattan and looked out on Wall Street and the old Customs House. I could see the Statue of Liberty and Ellis Island from the balcony. We were suing Continental Airlines, and they expected that I would be interrogated.

The lawyer, Rich Gresalfis, was fascinated with Henry's life and accomplishments. When we got closer to the deposition, Rich came to Florida to further prepare me and to look through papers in the office for discovery.

When it was time to go back home, Jeff took me to the Westchester Airport. On the plane I had another one of those attacks. It lasted for about an hour. I had an aisle seat and had to get up to allow the man sitting in the window seat to go to the rest room. It had been quieting down but then started all over again. Fortunately, it passed, or I would not have been able to get off the plane. It was the same fast pounding heartbeat, but when it was over, I was 100 percent, as though it had never happened.

With all my blessings I still had terrible bouts of depression. I thought about how I tried to help my mother when she was depressed. I told her to make two columns and to put her problems on one side and her blessings on the other. How very insensitive! I did not understand being old and being lonely then. I guess you cannot understand until it happens to you. I never knew the silence of loneliness. I did know, for me, the solution was to stay busy.

I had to complete the organization of Henry's office. It was complicated by the fact that he made multiple copies of everything, and I had to decide what I should keep and what I should discard. I had to get rid of all the file cabinets and turn it into a guest room. I found so many personal things in the file cabinets that would trigger bouts of tears.

I knew, too, that it would help to call friends and make dates, but that was an effort. I was in such a state of inertia. I did always find comfort in writing, so I wrote letters and poetry to Henry. Somehow, it helped.

My Crazy Thoughts

Where you are now—are you in a star?
What other worlds are beyond where we are?
Are there fluffy clouds and pearly gates?
Is there hell for those who hurt and hate?
Do you hear me when I call in the night?
The pennies that are shiny and bright,
Are you putting them there for me to find?
Or is my sorrow affecting my poor crazy mind?
Will I ever feel like a whole person again?
Will you be there as you promised
When I meet my end?

Chapter Fifty-four

Craig's Fiftieth Birthday Party

On November 1, David, Lisa and Zoe arrived. They were now living in Ashville, North Carolina. They had been to Boston for a memorial service for Lisa's mother, then to visit family in Connecticut and then to Disney. When they arrived at my door, Zoe looked like Tinker Belle in a sea green dress and her beautiful little self. I had arranged for them to stay in the condo next door.

David told me that even though Craig thought they were leaving on Saturday, there was going to be a surprise birthday party for Craig on Sunday night at Cathi and Bob Bates.' The plan was that Bob and Craig would be playing golf and when they arrived back at the Bates,' everyone would be there—Kathy's family, all the brothers and wives, many of the "Craig Gang" and, of course, Kyle and Courtney. The Bates' home is gorgeous with ten acres of beautiful grounds and fruit trees.

When Craig and Bob drove in, everyone was waiting on the driveway to greet him. It was indeed a surprise.

There was a tent with balloons and all kinds of posters, plus songs, speeches and poems for Craig. It was such a tribute to him, and he is so deserving.

After a sumptuous buffet dinner and birthday cake, we had a big bon fire. It was a great party, and I was overwhelmed in gratitude that my sons are so close and always there for each other. And all of them for Craig.

The first year without Henry was very hard for me, and my

emotions were like a seesaw. Sometimes I would sob for no real reason. Holidays were the worst and, even though Thanksgiving was wonderful at Faye and George's, I could not help reliving Thanksgiving of last year.

I struggled to stay busy and not to burden others with the tears of my broken heart, but on December 24 every one of my dear family called to help me through the day. Even Jill, whom I loved so much, called from New Zealand. We went to the candlelight service at church on Christmas Eve, and I could see him everywhere. I tried so hard to hold back the tears. On December 29, I wrote:

My dearest Henry

Today is a year since we put your body in the ground. It was the day my heart shattered into tiny pieces, and it will never be whole again. One year later, I look back at the wonderful life we had together and at the marvel of our love. I am feeling so alone without you. I keep seeking answers, and I know I will never find the answers. Not on this earth. Maybe beyond.

Though life was still a struggle, I sometimes felt ashamed that I was not more grateful. My family was so kind and loving to me, though there were health problems. David had a hip operation that thank God was successful, but I do not think he ever regained use of his arm after the shoulder surgeries.

Baby Jack needed to have his bladder repaired. It was hard for all of us, especially for Jon and Tara, but the surgery was amazing, and today Jack is a wonderful, healthy little boy.

Jill was exhausted from taking care of Ralph. She was confined to bed and had to put Ralph in a nursing home. We later found out that Jill had cancer of the bowel. I wanted so much to be with her, but she discouraged me from going to New Zealand when she died.

I wish Henry could be here to see our beautiful great grandchildren and to see Kyle graduate from the Charter school and from the Indian River Community College with an AA. We were all so proud of him. There was even an article about him on the first page of the "Press Journal." I wish Henry could have been there, but maybe he was! He had loved Kyle so much.

Henry was never out of my mind. I know he is happy wherever his soul has gone, and I just pray we will be together again, sometime, somewhere. I try to get on with life.

Once again, I turned to my art. This time, I did six stepping stones for the Turtletrax Mental Health Project, with the calligraphy for Love-Hope-Spirit-Faith-Respect and Patience. They were sold at auction.

Stepping Stones by Marcy Von Kohorn
Sold at auction for Mental Health

Continental Airlines, which we were suing for patent infringement for printing boarding passes, subpoenaed Craig and me for a deposition. It was scary, but Jamie and Rich thought it went well. We were then scheduled to be in court in Virginia in two months for a trial.

On March 31, I was supposed to be in court, but there was a last-minute settlement. It seems that the judge ruled in our favor about an important claim. I also learned that Continental was trying to disqualify me. The negotiations were complicated, but we finally settled for $700,000.

Chapter Fifty-five

The Henry Von Kohorn Trophy

An amazing thing happened at the tennis court one day. I was walking off the court after my game, when Dick Winkler approached me. He asked me if I would sponsor a tournament in honor of Henry. He was suggesting a donation to Habitat for Humanity of $1000. The Moorings Club had a wonderful charitable connection to Habitat for Humanity and had many volunteers building homes for the needy.

I had always wanted to do something to honor Henry. I told Dick I would get back to him. I came up with the idea that everyone in the family would contribute. I presented the plan to the family, and they were all thrilled with this tribute to Henry and to be a part of it.

A few days before the tournament on the weekend of Presidents Day in February, large signs appeared at the tennis court advertising "The Henry Von Kohorn Memorial Tennis Tournament sponsored by the Marcy Von Kohorn Family." It was also in the "Porthole," the club magazine. I was so proud that Henry was recognized for the love of the game and for his skill. There were pictures of him playing tennis and articles about the tournaments he'd won posted at the court. I never dreamed that he would be remembered in this way.

This has now become an annual event. I have played in the tournament and sometimes Craig and Kyle. Henry came the first year, and Ken played last year.

It was always followed with a magnificent cocktail party on Monday, with incredible food to celebrate the various events that took place to benefit Habitat for Humanity.

Many times, I find I am talking myself out of a kind of depression. It certainly has to do with loneliness and with having no purpose in life. I know the cure for this is to keep busy, and I have tried to do that.

I volunteer at Hospice House every Thursday from three to six o'clock. I sit at the front door to greet people and to help them. I also make sure they sign in and sign out when they leave. Hospice House is beautiful, and I have made many friends there with staff and with fellow volunteers. I received my five-year pin at the volunteer luncheon. It is also where my turtle, Florida Flo, stands at the front door.

I could play bridge every day, but in the three hours I sit there I could do a painting. I sometime look out the window at people hanging out at the pool, sunbathing, visiting or having wine together and wonder how they have nothing better to do with their time. I also wonder how women can talk to each other nonstop!

I also go to my Seekers group every Wednesday morning. This circle of friends that I meet with are bright and choose interesting subjects for discussion each week.

Then there are the concerts by the Atlantic Chamber Classical Orchestra with Maggie, Faye and Kathy every couple of months.

I also am active in the National League of American Pen Women. I am membership chairman of our Vero Beach Branch and have been a member of this professional group since 1970. The NLAPW is the oldest club for professional women in the arts in the country. Our headquarters are in Washington, D.C., with branches in almost every state in the US. I have been accepted as a member in art and in letters.

Summer days in Florida are steamy and rainy but so peaceful when the snow birds go home. I have gone on trips and usually go to visit family. One year, I spent some time with my good friend Maggie Johnston at her summer place in Essex. I carried some paintings with me, in hopes of interesting a gallery in my work. I was quite thrilled when the well-known Cooley Gallery in Old Lyme invited me to show some of my paintings at their famous Christmas show.

In summer the thunder is loud, angry and rumbling. I used to be afraid of thunder when I was a little girl. My mother would tell me that it was God in his golden chariot. Now the only fear I have is of the terrible hurricanes we have in Florida. I guess even Utopia is not perfect.

Life is good and even though I do not have anyone to share it with, I am grateful for friends and family. Of course, I will never stop missing Henry.

Marcy and Henry's Grandchildren

Marcy and her Six Sons

Chapter Fifty-six

My Birthday Party

On September 22, 2010, it was very damaging to my ego to know that I was turning 85 years old. I was discovering that "old age is not for sissies." I was grateful that I had no major health issues, except of course for diabetes, which I inherited from my grandmother Mollie. I do find, though, that I cannot do what I used to. To my chagrin, if I drop something on the floor, it takes a supreme effort to pick it up. Of course, I am always dropping things!

On the rare occasions that I have a dinner party, it takes a week to prepare and another week to recuperate.

I even have a problem putting on my shoes.

But even though I hate getting old, I received a wonderful and precious gift that made my heart sing and that made this day a page in my golden book of memories. All my sons were together to celebrate my birthday. How honored I felt and how grateful. It was a magical evening down at the pool. Craig and Kathy prepared a delicious barbeque dinner. It was such fun. Even the night sky was magic, with a bright moon, twinkling stars and a lovely breeze.

My dearest sister-in-law, Jill, died on August 11, 2011. It hardly seemed possible. She was so young, so vivacious, so creative, so beautiful and so very dear to all of us. She went quickly, and she was so brave. She was only sixty-eight years old. I will never stop missing her.

Ralph had died eight months before. He had been in failing health for a long time, and he must have been heartbroken to know that Jill had terminal cancer.

On May 25, Ken and Don (their family lawyer), John (Jill's brother) and I went to the family plot in Greenwich. The grave site was open, and Don lifted a box out of his suitcase that contained the ashes of Ralph and Jill and of their beloved cat Minky. The ashes were put in the ground and were covered with grass. Ken conducted a little ceremony; I recited the piece about the boat leaving the shore and arriving on the other side. We then went to a restaurant on Greenwich Avenue. Another trip down memory lane.

I was surprised when Steven and Karen (Ralph's son and daughter) arrived at the restaurant with his grandchildren Jacquie, Piers, and Marcus. I could not figure how they knew where we were, as we had selected the restaurant by random, but we were happy to see them. We added another table and enjoyed getting to know our Australian branch of the family.

I had a wonderful evening with Bob and Dana and my granddaughters Melody and Olivia. I stayed overnight with them, and the next morning we took a ride to see our old house on Pecksland Road. Could I ever have lived there with Henry and the children? It seemed like a different lifetime.

We went back to the cemetery so I could say goodbye to Henry, and then the entire family arrived and also our friends, the Wymans, to conduct a more formal service for Ralph and Jill.

Jeff and Elizabeth invited the family to their home for a beautiful reception. Everything was done so graciously, and the food was beautifully presented. Our whole family was there. Together with the Australian branch, we were a large and impressive family. We sat around talking to our new friends and family from down under until very late.

Kyle graduated from the University of North Florida in December. It seemed like yesterday I was wheeling him to the beach and feeding him in his little highchair. Kyle had worked at the Springhill Marriott during the summer while he was in high school. Because of this connection, he was able to apply for a job as operation manager at a hotel in Lake Charles, Louisiana. He did get the job, which was

Grandson Kyle

amazing as the economy was bad and jobs were hard to find. Before his graduation, he flew to Lake Charles to find a place to live. After the graduation weekend from college, he rented a "You Haul It" and moved directly to his new job. Craig drove with him and helped him settle in.

It was not the same without him on Christmas morning, but we had a technological miracle called Skype! The computer was on the coffee table, and there he was on the screen. We opened gifts together, laughed together and had a wonderful Christmas. Kyle was with us. He later became a realtor.

The little town of Vero Beach has something special about it. Aside from the wonderful climate, it has a first-class museum and theater. It is a tourist town and becomes something of a ghost town when the snow birds go North in the summer. It has culture and quiet dignity, which is why many people choose to live here all year around.

The Great Divide by Marcy Von Kohorn

Vero Beach has an art section where most of the galleries are located. Many are cooperative galleries which are owned by a group of artists who participate in the upkeep and sales. There is a sizable upfront fee to belong to these galleries. Very few galleries are owned and operated by one owner who selects the artists, hangs the art work and collects for the sales from which the artist is paid.

My medium is watercolor. When I moved to Vero Beach, I joined the Artist Guild which was a cooperative gallery, but I did not get along with some of the other members. I was a charter member and showed there for about five years. Everyone loved my flowers.

I then was accepted by the Director of the Rablen West Gallery as an artist, and I showed and sold my work there for about ten years, until the Gallery went out of business.

After that I mostly showed in Palm Beach, Orlando and Stuart, as there were not many galleries in Vero Beach.

When I learned that a gallery was opening with professional owners, I was anxious to show them my work. I made an appointment and took several of my paintings. I was thrilled when I was accepted and developed a very warm relationship with the owners of the Darby Gallery, Linda and George O'Malley. The gallery was outstanding because of the diversification of the work they showed. The styles were as varied as the artists themselves, and they featured a new artist every month. The artists had very impressive resumes and were different from each other. The only thing we had in common was "art."

When I explained Chinese brushstrokes, Linda saw the brushstrokes on the paintings I brought for her to see. When she and George came to my condo to see my work, they loved what they saw and invited me to do a show in April. I was thrilled with the space reserved for my work. My paintings looked wonderful on the walls. My waterlilies sold for $3300 at the opening.

The following day I did a demonstration. I sold all my demo pieces and donated the proceeds to the scholarship fund of the Vero Beach Art Club.

After each opening, Linda and George invited us to their beautiful home for pizzas, with an open bar. I loved those evenings and getting to know other artists, many of whom brought musical instruments to play some wild and wonderful music. I always knew there was a part of me that belonged to an unconventional and Bohemian place.

I was at every opening, the first Friday of every month. The owners encouraged me to raise my prices, and I sold many pieces. When the gallery closed, I missed the glamour and the exposure. I also missed my fellow artists. Part of the reason Linda and George closed the gallery was financial, but part was personal. When their grandson was four months old, the doctors discovered he had a heart problem. He was taken to the Joe DiMaggio Hospital in Florida where he was hooked up to an artificial heart and put on a wait list to receive a new heart. After a long wait, he did receive a new heart, and today, he is a beautiful little boy. His family is devoted to his care.

Twilight by Marcy Von Kohorn

Marcy in Peru

Chapter Fifty-seven

Peru

As I was packing to go on my trip to Peru, I wondered what crazy impulse made me decide to go to Machu Picchu. I had seen the brochure on a table at a party and had met Jaes through the Seekers. Jaes was a Shaman and was at the party. She was leading a group, and I had always felt close to her. I had made enough money from my art sales to pay for the trip, and it was a treat I was giving myself.

I kept a journal. On the first page I wrote "on my search for magic." It was not only a trip to another world, but I met such genuine and kind traveling companions, who became like extended family to me.

We met at the Ft. Lauderdale airport and flew directly to Lima, Peru, where we spent the night at a "no-star" hotel. My room was on the third floor. There was no elevator. It had a table and a bed. Wonderful, young, blue-eyed Nate carried my overnight bag up the steps for me and was at my door the next morning to take it downstairs.

A funny thing happened when we arrived at the Lima airport. I could not imagine why this adorable doggie was following me around. It so happens that I love my Fuji apples and had scattered a few of them in my suitcase. The trained dog sniffed my apples, so I was singled out to go to the inspector who removed two of them. The dog still followed me, so the inspector removed two more. He did miss a few! Everyone was good natured about this.

I found budding friendships. Nate was my hero and was always there to help.

In the morning, I grabbed a cup of coffee, and we boarded the bus to the airport where we flew to Cusco. We were taken to a very picturesque hotel. All the walls were of thick stone. There was a samovar of hot cocoa tea in the lobby, which was delicious and helpful with the high altitude. My single room was three large steps down. There was no hot water, and the room was very cold.

We all met to walk to a restaurant. The pavement was so narrow, it would have been easy to slip off into the road and in front of a car. I had to be very careful to hug the wall.

After dinner when we returned to the hotel, I could really feel the altitude and had palpitations. In addition, no matter what clothes I put on, I was still freezing cold. I was so grateful for the warm bed socks Kathy gave me for a going away present.

Sharon, one of my new friends, knocked on my door. When she saw how cold my room was, she called Jaes. Neither of them could turn on the radiator. Jaes was then able to get an electric radiator from the hotel, which made a huge difference.

In the morning, another of our group came to see me. Janette explained that she was a doctor and would be there for me if I needed help. She brought me a can of oxygen and showed me how to use it in case I got the altitude sickness again.

We met at the front door and boarded a plane to Paz y Luz where we stayed at a charming hotel, more like a guesthouse with a kitchen, beautiful gardens and a large summerhouse for us to hold our meetings. There was also a restaurant. My room was on the first floor, and every morning, I awoke to see the beautiful mountains in the mist. My room was sparse but comfortable, and at last I could unpack as we would be there for four days.

We met in the summerhouse for a spiritual and moving ceremony with two Shamans in native dress. They used bells and blessed each of us. After the ceremony, we stood around an open fire in silence.

Every evening we met in the summerhouse to talk about the next day's plans. We would end each day with a "check in" to share our thoughts and then, in a circle, hold hands and take a few quiet moments to reflect. More and more I felt a connection to my new friends.

The following day, we boarded a bus for the Sacred Valley. We walked up the mountain, and the view was breathtaking. We stopped at a plateau where water was streaming down the side of the mountain, and we had a little ceremony with Angel, our Shaman on this trip. The group went on to climb to the top of the mountain, which they thought would be too steep for me coming down, so I agreed to meet them later in a small town at the bottom of the mountain at a café.

Angel drove me to the little village, and I happily explored while waiting for my companions. My first priority was to find a phone center to call Craig since I had not checked in since I left.

A small boy named Pedro kept following me. I spoke a little Spanish, so I asked him to take me to a phone center. He led me to the phone center and helped me to tell the attendant what I wanted. I dialed with the country code 001 and Craig answered. Just the sound of his voice made me want to cry. It was so good to talk to him. I guess I was homesick.

Pedro then walked me back to the café. I gave him two dollars and bought some of the wooden toy birds he was selling.

I waited at the café for the group to arrive. They were late. I guess the climb took longer than they thought. My little friend Pedro kept peeping in to check on me.

After dinner, we all went shopping. I bought some small gifts to take home. I found a purple llama for Melody. Since she had been a child, she'd talked about a purple llama. What a find!

When we arrived back at Paz y Luz, the sky was like black velvet, with a crescent moon and huge bright stars. There was mist arising from the mountain like white clouds. Music like an echo surrounded me, probably from a festival somewhere. It was like another world— a magical and a spiritual one—and I was part of it all.

On Monday, the bus picked us up. It was raining, but just a fine drizzle. The mountains looked like a Chinese painting.

We stopped at a sacred place, and our Shaman said some prayers and gave us each some "San Pedro." It was supposed to alter the consciousness. It made me feel very relaxed, and the beauty of my surroundings touched me even more.

We drove to the top of the mountain where we stopped at a magnificent old church. We first passed through a small sanctuary.

One by one, we each put our hand into a niche where there was a large red stone. We were told to make a wish. I wished that the hand that I put on that stone could paint the beauty I had seen that day.

The cathedral was very old and full of holiness. One of my new friends, Melissa, was said to be a psychic. She came to me and told me she could sense Henry there and that he wanted me to know he was always with me. She and I hugged and, whether it was the San Pedro or Melissa, I did feel Henry's presence. We left through a small shrine where there was an altar, and I lit candles for my loved ones.

Once again, back at Paz y Luz, we had "check in," and I was made to feel like a cherished part of our circle of friendship.

That day, for some strange reason, I thought about Brandy, the Saint Bernard we had in Hartsdale when David and Bob were small children. I did not walk David and Bob to the school bus at the end of our driveway one day. I still feel guilty, after all these years. Brandy followed David and got under the wheel of the bus and was killed. The children would no longer go to school on the bus with the driver who accidentally ran over him. This was a place where animals have spirits, and maybe Brandy was forgiving me, even though it was over fifty years ago.

We stopped at a large rock formation where the east wind blew through the large crevice to join the west wind as the light filtered in from the top of the rock. The spirits whispered in the wind. In the passageway between the boulders was a large flat slab. Our Shaman told us that it was where young virgins were sacrificed to appease the gods. Puma and Roberto, our Shamans, held a ceremony for us and gave us our first San Pedro of the day. The drink made me feel relaxed and, between that and the altitude, I did not have much energy. We stopped on the road at a public restroom. It was very primitive. Somehow, I managed to lock myself inside. I pounded on the door until the group realized I was missing. It really was scary until they found the key. A few minutes later, Catherine did the same thing.

We then went on to see the ancient ruins. I managed to climb pretty far up, wandering through the stones and the rocks. It was hard to believe that families once lived in these structures centuries ago. I found it very beautiful.

Our last stop was a large meadow, connected by steps to a series of grassy plateaus, each with a waterfall originating from the top where there was a huge spring feeding the rushing water which traveled down to the meadows below.

We left by bus to return to Cusco. At the hotel, I had the same room that reminded me of a dungeon, but at least this time there was an electric heater so that it was more comfortable.

The next morning at breakfast, I began to have palpitations and headed to a chair to rest. Janette noticed that I was having a problem and was there again with the oxygen. As I inhaled it, all the symptoms disappeared. We boarded the bus to Sacsaywaman.

As we arrived, there was a strange wind storm. Walking up the mountainside, we came to a flat area where there were huge rock formations, almost like pyramids. I had to wonder how they got there as it would have been humanly impossible to move these majestic boulders up the mountain. As I walked further, I saw llamas grazing in a grassy meadow. I sat down on a rock and meditated as I soaked in the magnificence of this peaceful and magical place.

Our final trip was to Machu Picchu. We took the bus to the train station at six in the morning and boarded the very slick and luxurious train. Hostesses came around offering us drinks and snacks. It was well done, and the scenery was indescribably beautiful with the mist hugging the mountaintops and patches of fog floating through the trees.

The hotel in Machu Picchu was lovely. I was assigned to a large and comfortable room with a beautiful view of the mountains.

After lunch we went up the mountain by bus. There were lots of sharp turns and narrow roads. Our Shaman, Angel, explained the many sites to us as we traveled.

The mountain was steep but so beautiful. Now on foot, I made it up, though sometimes I felt I could not take another step. We stopped at the Temple of the Sun and many mystical spots where I could look down and take in the curves and valleys of where I had been.

Almost to the very top, we looked out and saw a storm approaching. Carla, another one of my new friends, quickly took my arm and said that we must hurry down the mountain as the stones get slippery in the rain. We barely made it down before the storm hit.

Back in the bus, leaving Machu Picchu, the sun came out, and there was an exquisite rainbow to end our day.

Our hotel was in a charming little village, and the next day I explored and went to the shops and to the marketplace.

Leaving by train, we walked over the bridge to the railroad station. The train was modern, and the scenery was gorgeous. I sat with a nice couple from Connecticut. He was a professor at UConn.

Back in the hotel in Cusco, where this time my accommodations were roomy and comfortable, Jaes called a meeting which was to be our last "check in." We formed a circle and, holding hands, felt the sadness of our parting but also the lasting bond of our friendship. Back home, I sent Nate an email to thank him for all he had done for me. He returned an email to me saying, "Thank you for being such a wonderful elder, so young at heart, so joyful and grateful, smart, funny and full of joy. I know you touched everyone's heart, including mine." Remember what Puma said: "Today is the best day of your life." I had found mystery in the mountains, and I had found love and friendship. And, yes, I did find the magic I was searching for.

Mist in the Mountains by Marcy Von Kohorn

Chapter Fifty-eight

Melody's Wedding

I went to see Henry and Meredith's new home in Princeton. Vero Beach now has our own airline called Elite Airlines. I boarded at the airport on Aviation Boulevard and landed at the Newark airport, non-stop. It was like door-to-door service.

Their new house had the same charm as the one they had left in Westport. It was smaller and close enough to town that they could walk to most places. Meredith did a great job decorating.

We went to the University, which has changed some since Henry was an undergraduate. Henry was still involved in many volunteer programs. It was a good move for them. There are enough bedrooms for Isabelle and Josh with the children, and Emily and Nate and their two children. There are interesting programs, concerts and lectures for them to enjoy.

Henry drove me to Connecticut for Melody's wedding to Todd Russell. The October wedding was perfect in every way. Even the weather cooperated. Melody was a beautiful bride, and it was a touching ceremony. Her sister, Olivia, was lovely as her attendant. Bob and Dana were proud of their little family, as well they should be.

Melody

I had a hard time holding back the tears and felt blessed that everyone in the family was there.

When my six handsome sons posed for a picture, it was a picture that will remain in my heart forever.

My oldest son, Henry, turned 70—hard to believe, and I went to his birthday party. They had 60 guests for a casual outdoor cookout. The Tiger Lilies sang, and Isabelle joined in as she used to sing with them. I spent time with all my great grandchildren and even got some warm snuggles.

And my youngest son Craig just turned 60. It all happened so fast. It was amazing.

Marcy and her Great Grandchildren

Chapter Fifty-nine

My Ninetieth Birthday

Then on September 22, 2015, I turned 90 years old.

My birthday party was unbelievable. It started down at the pool. From my window, I could look down at the elaborate decorations, all in yellow, and everyone dressed in yellow. (Can you guess? Yellow is my favorite color.) That sure made me smile and glad I was wearing a yellow skirt.

We had drinks and snacks around the pool and dinner in the party room, all prepared and served by caterers. The food was incredible. There were 43 family members and a few special friends.

What I will never forget was the speeches from my sons—witty, loving and praise that I felt was undeserved but touched my heart.

I never expected to be celebrated this way and was overwhelmed with all the cards, gifts, flowers and calls, and at the outpouring of love. Underneath this person I call "me," I do not feel worthy, but I was bursting with gratitude.

I scheduled time to give an art demonstration for all the children. I was so pleased that I had the attention of each one of them. Even the youngest seemed focused watching me paint.

It went off better than I could imagine, and it was a way of bonding with my great grandchildren, each one so precious.

My family keeps growing. To think it all started with Henry and me, and now, between weddings and babies, we are really multiplying.

My very special granddaughter, Courtney, graduated from

college and became a teacher—no doubt a very good one. Shortly after, she announced her engagement to Chris Hodum. He proposed at a family party. It was very romantic.

Courtney and Chris were then married in a lovely rustic outdoor setting on November 26, 2016. Pastor Jack performed the ceremony. Courtney was a beautiful bride and (only Courtney would be so thoughtful) she had a small table set up with a photo of Henry right next to an assigned seat for me. Courtney and Chris made a handsome couple.

My wonderful Emily married Nate Shanok on July 15, 2015. She had been with him in Istanbul, where he was sent by his company to open a new office. The ceremony was held at Henry and Meredith's home on the fresh green lawn, bursting with flowers and summer shrubs.

Ken married Dana June 6, 2015. This time he got it right. It was a beautiful wedding at their country club in Connecticut.

Love was in the air!

Although I am now walking with a cane, I went to a conference in Daytona Beach for the National League of American Pen Women and found such comradery with the members, who all came from Florida. When I enter the world of creativity, it fills my heart with joy. I seem to have so much in common with these ladies. I went with my good friend Rosemary Brofos, president of our branch and with Joan Foster.

In 2015, I won second prize in a Pen Women poetry contest for a poem named "Sunset." At this conference, I was awarded three certificates, one for my four-act play, "The In Vitro World" and one for my short story, "Florida Flo" and for my poem, "The Fallen Bird." I was quite surprised.

In August we went on a cruise to Alaska on the Holland America line. It was Craig and Kathy, my friend Maggie with her daughter-in-law Cathy and me.

I used a cane but sometimes it was easier to push me in a wheelchair. My foot is numb from neuropathy, and an MRI of my back is very discouraging, but that did not stop us. Pushing the wheelchair was part of the fun (and faster).

Boarding the plane with Craig and Kathy to Seattle even gave us some advantages, as we were able to pre-board.

In Seattle, we walked to a liquor store to pick up a few bottles of red wine. Pushing me up and down the hills there and back was hilarious, and we all started giggling. Boarding the ship was hectic but being handicapped made it far easier for the three of us.

My stateroom was nice and roomy, and stepping out on my balcony I could watch the white foam of the waves and the gorgeous scenery. I had a running slide show of every mountain I could imagine and every painting I would like to do. God is after all the best artist, and I was in heaven.

Craig and Kathy had the adjoining stateroom. I was totally spoiled with my bacon and eggs and hot coffee served to me in my room.

Every day we found something interesting to do onboard the ship. Cocktail hour was red wine and snacks in my stateroom and on to a divine dinner. We had a table at the window and sometimes were able to spot a whale. After dinner there was an entertaining show in the auditorium, and on the way back to the cabin a stop at the roulette table. Craig and I won with number 22, but of course gave it all back.

The ship made several stops, and we sometimes chose the "excursion," but mostly we explored on our own. In Juno we boarded a boat to go whale watching, but it was a cloudy, misty day, and we only saw a few whales in the distance. In Sitka, Craig and Kathy went off on a hiking and bicycle tour and loved it. Maggie, Cathy, and I went on a tour bus and then found a little seafood restaurant where we pigged out on a bucket of crab legs.

The only trouble with the cruise is that it went too quickly. It was hard to get back to reality.

Chapter Sixty

Stem Cell Therapy

One day I was glancing through a magazine and noticed an ad for Stem Cell Therapy. The provider was called RBI and was located on 37th Street in Vero Beach. I knew enough about stem cell therapy to want to know more. The process of harvesting the cells which are in the body to help with healing makes sense to me.

I went to the Center and met with Jason, whom I clicked with right away and was even more convinced. It was costly. My doctors all said I was wasting my money, but I guess I do believe in Tinker Belle.

I waited a long time until I was contacted and went for my treatment at four o'clock that day. Jason was in charge of the entire program. Before beginning I was introduced to Dr. Portel who is a well-known anesthesiologist in our area. He would be injecting the stem cells. I was taken into the back room where the specialists collected my stem cells. There was then a long wait as the cells needed to be separated and to be purified.

The doctor then, with the help of an x-ray machine and my MRI, injected the cells back into my body. I was really excited when he said, "I have the needle right where your stenosis is and am releasing the cells there." I was supposed to start seeing some results in four months. Did it work? In April I definitely had a sense of well-being, but my neuropathy did not go away, and I still had a problem walking. Neuropathy comes from a damaged nerve which I doubt can be reversed.

It's hard to tell. Perhaps I could have been worse if I had not had it at all.

That summer we had a mandatory evacuation because Irma, a category five hurricane, looked like it might hit us. I wrapped each painting in plastic to protect them, closed the storm shutters, packed a bag and turned off the water.

I picked up my friend Miriam Hodges, and we went to Craig and Kathy's house on the mainland to be safe. Craig had just had back surgery, and it seemed to work, but in securing the house he probably was not being careful. It took time to heal. A category five to me was unimaginable, and I was frightened. That was a monster storm.

During the night, I could not sleep and watched the weather channel as Irma approached our coast line. Maybe it does pay to pray. At the last minute, the hurricane missed us, and we just had a very bad storm. We did, of course, lose power. Craig had a generator, so we did not leave there until we were told the elevator was working again at the condo.

In the summer of 2016, I had a show at the Emerson Center. I sold a painting, and the buyer then came to my condo to choose a companion piece.

In 2017, I had a show at a wonderful old house called the Spiritual Center. Linda and George hung that show for me. I showed 18 paintings, a few quite large. Hanging is an art, and they are pros. The show looked great.

Craig ended up at the door directing traffic as there were over 100 guests forming a line outside. It was a good opening, and I did sell some of my work.

It was close to the end of the year, and close to that terrible night of December 24 when I lost Henry. There is a saying, "The Lord giveth and the Lord taketh" and this day Courtney had a beautiful little baby boy, my great grandson Cayson, born on the same date I lost Henry in 2006.

Emily had baby Eleanor Mae (Nora), born in Istanbul and an adorable roly-poly dimpled baby boy named Henry (Hank).

And Melody had three beautiful baby girls. I now had 16 great grandchildren.

On Saturday, May 5, 2018, Kyle and Jessica got married in a

beautiful ceremony, again conducted by our wonderful Pastor Jack. The setting was exquisite with a large expanse of green lawn and flowering trees.

Tears came to my eyes as I saw the way Kyle looked at his lovely bride walking down the aisle to join him. I thought of my mother who told me, "God is Love."

Dee and Karen came from Australia for the wedding. Henry and Meredith arranged for a private room at a restaurant on the beach the night before the wedding. All the brothers and their families were there and also Dee and Karen. It was a great reunion and again the happiness of seeing my sons together.

Craig and Kathy had an open house on Sunday, and Monday the bride and groom left for their honeymoon to Saint Croix. It was such a joyful wedding weekend.

I had some health problems, but being old is not easy, and I seemed to wake up with a new ailment every day. Not only was I breaking down, but so were the appliances and the air conditioner. We were all getting old, but as Craig always says, "It is what it is," and I think the big secret is "to accept what cannot be changed."

Journey of Hope by Marcy Von Kohorn

Chapter Sixty-one

My Journey's End

The last few miles of my journey are still ahead of me, the ending just as unknown as the beginning.

Looking back at just a month until my 93rd birthday, I know I am old. I have been fortunate that I am still writing and painting. Inside I feel young.

I think of life as a classroom and have learned many lessons. I think I still have lessons to learn and things I need to do.

If I have learned anything, it is not to be afraid to leave myself open to life, to people and to the experience of living.

When Henry died, I felt my life was over. It was with great effort that I told myself, when I did not want to face another day without him, that I could make it a happy day, or I could stay unhappy. It was up to me, and being unhappy would not bring him back. I learned to count my blessings.

In my prayers, I asked God to give some meaning to my life. I no longer had someone to touch me, to hold my hand, to encourage me. I had no one to feel close to, to tell a secret to, or to tell me when to stop painting. I had no purpose to my life.

It was then I realized how much I still had to give.

Whenever I could find someone in need, I found happiness in reaching out. The real message is to do something for someone without the need for thanks. The ego does get in the way for all of us. It is human.

Goodness is its own reward, and evil is its own punishment. I have seen that selfishness, unkindness and meanness poison the soul. The greedy get greedier. Those who have not learned to give of themselves can never find happiness. And it is true that money cannot buy contentment.

I am hoping that this book will become a treasure for my family, to be passed on to generations to come, and that my readers will have found some interest in sharing my life's experiences.

Although parts of it are sad, there are all the colors of my palette intertwined in the joy of my painting that has made my heart sing. I have invited you into my own small art studio that is such a private place for me. I have also given you some glimpses into my soul.

I think my life has had a rainbow of colors though it often followed rain drops. There is a balance in which we must all find our own peace.

As I am in the time of life that approaches the end, I believe because I have known love, I will know how to die, and that, if I live in someone's memory, I will live forever. I feel a sense of mortality in that my paintings will live on beyond me.

Mine has been a long and wonderful journey. I know now that I have followed a destiny laid out for me. I think that my great grandmother who told me that God wrote my life in a big golden book was right after all.

Poppies by Marcy Von Kohorn

A Late Bloomer

Published previously in The Pen Woman Magazine

I am almost ninety-three years old. I am a late bloomer, so I am really just getting started. I put off writing a book for so long, and I finished it yesterday. I guess I am late in everything. I get up late and get my energy in the late afternoon. I am usually inspired to write by 10:30 p.m. and try but never seem to get to bed before midnight. Sometimes I wake up with a poem. I jot it down and go back to sleep to work on it the next day.

I have always been a late bloomer. It took two tries to meet the right man. We were married for fifty years and without Henry I would never have been on time for anything.

Once I was painting a *po mo* on 3 gold boards and as usual lost track of time.

A *po mo* is pouring the paint onto the rice paper boards and letting it settle in a pattern that can end up as an abstract or maybe realism. I do Chinese watercolor and learned from my famous Chinese master, Diana Kan.

We were due out for dinner with friends, and Henry was scolding me. "Do you have any idea what time it is? Stop now!" What a bad time to stop, but of course he was right, and so I left the painting as it was, far from finished. When I returned home from our dinner date, I found the fairies had worked on it. The colors dried in a most amazing texture. I call the painting "In the Beginning," and it is not for sale.

Henry is gone. He died in 2006, and I will never stop missing him. Now I am on my own, and it is not easy. I walk with a walker as I have neuropathy, and that does slow me down, so I usually end up eating dinner at about 8:00 p.m. and always rush to cook something. Of course, when Henry was still with me, he sat in his chair watching me prepare what he called a gourmet meal. We ate to the music of Johanne Strauss Jr., but come to think of it, no matter how hard I tried, we never ate before 7:00. Henry just put up with me because we were in love.

When I lost him, I had to make up my mind to live. It took a long time before I could convince myself that he would never come back, though there were signs of him everywhere. He promised to leave me pennies, and I found them in the least expected places.

I had to convince myself though that being unhappy and avoiding friends was not going to help anyone. I had a huge and wonderful family of six sons—three born from my womb and three born in my heart. I have six daughters-in-law that I love, eleven grandchildren and seventeen great grandchildren. I had to count my blessings. I guess "what cannot be cured must be endured." Happiness is a state of mind.

I live in a condo, and it is almost like having an extended family. Last week I went downstairs to get in the car and the battery was dead. I had to go back to my condo to get the phone number of my friend I was meeting for lunch to ask her to pick me up. While waiting for her, Phil came along, and when I told him my tale of woe, he said, "Never mind, I will charge your battery for you and also fix your flat tire." I hadn't noticed the flat tire, but I was grateful to have a hero. Not only was my car running again, but this great guy followed me to Goodyear and later took me back there to pick up the car. Condo living is great.

We even have an angel who delivers the newspapers to our door in the morning. Her name is Gert.

When I want to go to the market, I walk to my car, open the back seat, fold up my walker and "furniture walk" to the front seat and drive. When I get there, I watch and wait for a grocery cart left in the parking lot and use it as a walker. When I get home with my groceries, I exchange my walker for a grocery cart. I take the groceries upstairs, take the empty cart down and collect the walker again.

It takes supreme effort for me to pick something up from the floor. I don't know why I keep dropping things. If I weren't such a neatnik I would just leave them there.

Last week, I went to the administration building to renew my handicap placard. I had to wait about a half hour to find a parking space. I took my walker out of the car and went in the building prepared with an application in hand which the doctor had filled out for me. That took a while because the nurse put in the wrong information about the doctor's medical number and had to change it. When I finally found someone to direct me, she informed me that they could not give me a new placard as the doctor had used white-out on the application. I had to present a new application.

When I went to renew my driver's license, I went online to be sure I took all the information required. I arrived at the administration building with my driver's license, my birth certificate, my marriage license and proof of residence. The same woman at the entrance looked at my credentials and informed me that I would also need my marriage license to my first husband. Was she kidding? Who would keep that?

The next time I went, I was armed with my license, every passport I ever had—valid or not—my graduation diploma, my baptismal certificate and proof of residence. This time there was a nice man on duty. He laughed and said, "Put all your papers away. I just need your license and passport." So far so good. I waited in line until one of the women who issues new licenses was ready. She called out, "Next," and so I walked to her station. Her expression was so stern that I told myself, "Don't celebrate yet." I wondered what would happen to her face if she smiled.

I passed the vision test.

She then asked me, "Who was here with me?" I answered, "No one." She asked, "How did I get there?" I answered, "I drove here." She then asked to see my registration and insurance papers. When she seemed satisfied with those, she informed me that because I use a walker, I would have to take a driving test. "Okay," I agreed. She advised me to call someone to be with me and cautioned me that if I failed the test, she would be obliged to take away my license.

I thought about calling my son away from his office and answered her, "I'm ready, thank you."

She watched me as I folded up my walker and put it in the back seat. She then got in the passenger seat next to me with the test papers on her lap. She instructed me to drive straight ahead to the stop light and turn right to go to the course designated for the test. I was so nervous that I realized I made that turn without putting on my turn signal. Strike number 1. She asked me how I would park on a hill. I don't ever remember a hill in Florida but realized too late that I forgot to say turn your wheels in. Later she told me that I also did not say to turn the engine off before I got out of the car. I failed the part where she told me to make a turn without doing a U-turn. I made the turn properly in three movements but used my side mirrors instead of turning my head around.

I parked in a tight space and forgot to put my turn signal on.

This lady was out to get me—but surprise—I passed the test!

Old age is not for sissies, and I have decided not to be a sissy. I am lucky that I always seem to have a project. It gives me a reason to get out of bed in the morning.

It is all in the mind.

As my dear friend Burton said many years ago when he was dying of multiple sclerosis, "Nothing is good or bad. It is thinking that makes it so."

I am thinking at ninety-three that life is great as long as you have your health. The small inconvenience of needing a walker is no problem.

I will just keep plugging along and enjoying what years I have left. I know I am near the end, but because I am a late bloomer and always late, I probably will be late in that, too.

My Parting Prayer

I knew when I saw you slipping away
That it was the end
But I did not know how forever
The end would be.

I knew when I cradled you in my arms
That it was the end
I cried
I knew I would never see you again.

And now I too will be slipping away
I hope we will meet in life everlasting
And who knows at the end
Maybe the Journey begins all over again.

—end—

CPSIA information can be obtained
at www.ICGtesting.com
Printed in the USA
BVHW022044240619
551798BV00018B/628/P